A CRY FOR CHARACTER

DARY MATERA

HOW A GROUP OF STUDENTS CLEANED UP THEIR ROWDY SCHOOL AND SPAWNED A WILDFIRE ANTIDOTE TO THE COLUMBINE EFFECT

Prentice
Hall Press

Library of Congress Cataloging-in-Publication Data

Matera, Dary
    A cry for character : how a group of students cleaned up their rowdy school and
spawned a wildfire antidote to outrageous behavior / by Dary Matera.
      p. cm.
    ISBN 0-7352-0272-9
    1. Moral education—United States—Case studies. 2. Mundelein High School
(Mundelein, Ill.)—Case studies. I. Title.
LC311.M35 2001
370.11′4—dc21
                                       2001021323
                                            CIP

ATTENTION: CORPORATIONS AND SCHOOLS

Prentice Hall Press books are available at quantity discounts with bulk purchase for
educational, business, or sales promotional use. For information, please write to:
Prentice Hall Special Sales, 240 Frisch Court, Paramus, New Jersey 07652. Please
supply: title of book, ISBN, quantity, how the book will be used, date needed.

Cover Photo

Mundelein High School's Class of 1999 was among the school's initial group of
underclassmen to go through the trailblazing First Class Character Education program
that was developed and taught by students from the Class of 1998. Pictured are some of
the finalists for the 1998-99 Homecoming Court. From left, Misty Blue, Ryan Nally,
Marit Johnson, Beth Hamm, Rachel Serio, Mike Henning, Maryann Ranchero, Elena
Pagan, Greg Pannhausen, and Kim Hofert. **Credit: Maryann Ranchero**

**Prentice
Hall Press** Paramus, NJ 07652

http://www.phdirect.com

ACKNOWLEDGMENTS

Special thanks to Sharon Zasadil of the mighty class of 1973 for all her help and photos; Mary Ann Ranchero for her help, spirit, and cover photo; Mike Koehler, Karen Royer, Coach John Ahlgrim, Tee Newbrough, John Davis, John Scornavacco, Scott Kasik, Bob Gottlieb, Tammy A. Linn, and all the students, faculty members, parents, and administrators who helped make this book happen.

Much appreciation to Patricia Likens and Laura Penny of the Arizona Department of Education, Jake Phillips of Empower America, Charles Haynes of The Freedom Forum, and Esther F. Schaeffer of The Character Education Partnership.

Thanks to M.N. Susan, of the Wagner High Falcons, Class of '72 for her crack Internet research assistance.

Extra special thanks to my editor at Prentice Hall Press, Debora Yost, without whom this would not have happened.

Thanks for editorial assistance go to Fran Matera, Ph.D., The Walter Cronkite School of Journalism and Telecommunication, Arizona State University, and Denise Estfan, M.A., for additional Internet research.

TABLE OF CONTENTS

It was supposed to be fun and games, but when this photo of 1996 Mundelein High Homecoming Queen Megan Happ appeared in the local newspaper, it caused quite a stir. The photo of the pudding-smeared senior came to symbolize a high school out of control. The wild homecoming assembly involved a rather unique, and some say vulgar, method of selecting the queen. (Credit—Todd Heisler, Pioneer Press)

PROLOGUE

A BLIGHT OF VIOLENCE STAGGERS AMERICA'S SCHOOLS

On the morning of April 20, 1999, two twisted teenagers accomplished what a rash of school shootings, rampant vandalism, myriad teacher assaults, plummeting test scores, and a stadium full of alarmed educators had failed to achieve. The pair grabbed the world by the throat and forced it to confront the reality of what was happening inside the American public education system.

In an era where guns in the classroom have become all too common, these high school seniors upped the ante to a startling degree. They brought 76 homemade pipe bombs and other assorted explosives to school that day, along with a TEC-DC9 9mm semiautomatic handgun, a Stevens, double-barrel, sawed-off 12-gauge shotgun, a 9mm Hi-Point semiautomatic carbine, and a Savage-Springfield, 12-gauge sawed-off pump shotgun. To feed the hungry weapons, they lined hundreds of shells and bullets in neat, shiny rows inside specialized utility belts. Gritty match strikers were taped to their forearms, no doubt to light the bombs that they concealed in duffel bags and stuffed inside backpacks and ammunition pouches. Just in case things got a bit tight, they were prepared to unsheathe any of four separate knives.

To shield their munitions, the militaristic duo sported long black trench coats. The ominous fashion statement was completed by a shared pair of black gloves—possibly as some kind of Kamikaze blood-brother death bond.

The distressed but determined assailants walked toward their familiar campus at 11:19 A.M. and began blasting away, eventually ripping off an astounding 188 shots and exploding 30 bombs. When the smoke cleared 16 minutes later, 12 classmates and one teacher lay dead or dying, and 23 students were injured. The death toll rose to 15 a chaotic 33 minutes later when the attackers turned their guns on themselves in the library. It was the worst school-shooting spree in U.S. history.

Most people remember bits and pieces of these much-publicized details. What few recall is how deeply the two youths bungled their original mission. Eric Harris and Dylan Klebold were distressed that morning at Columbine High School in Littleton, Colorado, because their grand scheme of apocalyptic destruction had actually fallen apart. Two massive, 20-pound propane bombs stashed in the cafeteria failed to detonate. If they had, authorities believe that 488 people in the bustling lunchroom would have perished, as well as 56 who were quietly studying in the library one floor above.

The unexpected snafu forced Eric and Dylan to shift to plan B: the random, one-by-one shooting of anybody unfortunate enough to cross their path.

In the aftermath, everyone from politicians to educators to newspaper columnists was quick to place the blame on the "usual suspects." Conservatives and church groups pointed fingers at the liberals, atheists, and pagans for loosening the reins of school discipline, tying the hands of teachers and administrators, and taking God, prayer, and religious-based morals out of schools. This, they argued, left students like Eric Harris and Dylan Klebold without an ethical compass or a shred of conscience. The liberals fired back that it was actually the conservatives and their strident, one-path Christian religion, their success-based social elitism, centuries of favoritism shown to the dominant white race, and unhealthy competition for academic and athletic honors that alienated and enraged a pair of outcasts like Eric and Dylan. Educators weighed in with various complaints of their own, blaming the tragedy on every pet agenda possible, from underfunded schools to low teacher salaries. Newspaper and television pundits had a field day picking and choosing among all these politically based, hot-button issues.

Part of the confusion was that Eric and Dylan themselves didn't provide a coherent clue to their motives. Although the teens left behind rambling suicide notes, diaries, and video tapes, they were mostly a mishmash of blanket racism, rebellion, and hate combined with overtones of a class struggle. Their bold and savage act was intended to "kick-start a revolution" that in reality was intellectually vague and unspecified. "If you could see all the anger I've stored over the past four (obscenity) years," Klebold exclaimed in a video without going into clarifying detail or even completing his sentence. The former Boy Scout, Little League pitcher, and computer whiz instead snarled about some routine sibling rivalry regarding a popular jock brother, and expressed typical teenage angst against the "stuck up" in-crowd at school. Harris, who played soccer and collected baseball cards as a child, railed against the mobile, military brat lifestyle that forced him to change schools frequently and always be the new kid "at the bottom of the ladder."

"I'm going to kill you all," Klebold announced. Despite the inherent weaknesses that plagued his motive and reasoning, he had tried to do just that.

In an aside that fed the fires of those who like to shift the blame away from schools and toss it on the ever-convenient, whipping-boy entertainment industry, Eric and Dylan gleefully mentioned how famous directors like Steven Spielberg and Quentin Tarantino would be fighting over their story. The seniors assured themselves that although they wouldn't be alive to reap the laurels of their demented act, they would nevertheless achieve that ultimate American dream of becoming famous.

From a sociological standpoint, one of the most disturbing aspects of the Columbine massacre is the team effort displayed by these misfits. History is full of lone-wolf psychos going off the deep end and committing atrocities. Rarely, however, have two teenagers plotted a mass murder/suicide of this magnitude together, met with initial failure, regrouped, and then carried out an intense, ad-libbed alternate plan without panicking, breaking form, or giving in to the survival instinct. What was going on in their world, or more specifically, in their school, that caused two separate identities to leap, hand-in-shared-glove-hand, into such an unprecedented abyss of violent insanity? Whatever the argumentative, politically charged theories, the answers seem to lie squarely inside what many see as the crumbling of the American public education system.

As a final creepy, but telling, touch, Harris, a fan of dark, carnage-packed video games like "Doom," promised that the evil of April 20 would cross into another dimension. He and his dead buddy would stalk their surviving classmates as ghosts and "drive them insane." That prediction took on a chilling, ethereal meaning less than a year later when a series of additionally shocking events rocked the already scarred Littleton community. On February 1, 2000, the frozen body of an eleven-year-old fifth grader named Antonio Davalos was found inside a trash bin two blocks north of Columbine High. The boy had been strangled and stuffed inside a duffel bag. (A family friend was later arrested and charged with the murder.)

Two weeks after the Davalos incident, Columbine students Nick Kunselman, 15, and Stephanie Hart, 16, were gunned down under mysterious circumstances inside a Subway Sandwich Shop where Kunselman worked. It was less than an hour after midnight on St. Valentine's Day, and Stephanie was visiting her boyfriend as he closed up. An unidentified gunman, possibly another teen, waltzed in and killed the young couple for reasons only the assailant knows. Police have been stymied in their investigation.

Eight days later, a man sitting in a parked car shot himself in the head during a suicide attempt a block from the Subway Shop where Kunselman and Hart died. Moments afterward, Columbine student Erin Walton unknowingly pulled her car over to pick up some friends from a nearby shopping plaza. Erin arrived in time to see the police drag the man's bloody body from his car. She promptly fainted. In yet another ironic twist, Erin had not only been inside the school when Eric and Dylan unleashed their massacre, she was the subsequent victim of an Internet threat from a Florida teen who sent her an AOL instant messenger note that he was going to "finish what begun." The communication closed the nervous campus for two days and traumatized the sensitive Erin even further. (The Florida teen, a high school drama student named Michael Campbell, was simply horsing around. However, in what many observers outside Colorado saw as extreme overkill, he was shipped to Denver, convicted of sending a threat across state lines, and sentenced to four months in a federal prison.)

The horror didn't stop there. Three months later, Columbine's star basketball player, Greg Barnes, inexplicably committed suicide. His parents and mental health experts blamed the more acceptable "post-traumatic stress syndrome," rather than some ghostly influence. Yet, in a sense, post-traumatic stress syndrome can be viewed as a psychiatric way of describing a very real manifestation of Harris and Klebold's beyond-the-grave curse. Either way, Barnes didn't leave a suicide note, thereby offering no clue as to why a popular young athlete bound for college on a full athletic scholarship decided to hang himself in his garage.

To the residents of Littleton, Colorado—and to the people across America reading about it in the newspaper—the madness seemed unending. Unfortunately, the truth presented by studying the bigger picture is actually even more frightening. Columbine was little more than a peak on a recent flow chart of what has been happening in American schools.

Most baby boomers who grew up in the 1950s, '60s, '70s and '80s cannot recall reading about, much less experiencing, a single shooting incident at an American secondary educational facility. The infamous tragedy at Kent State University in 1970—where the National Guard fired upon a group of Vietnam war protestors, killing four—sticks in everyone's mind because it was such a shocking rarity. In contrast, consider that the National School Safety Center recorded 236 homicides and suicides on school campuses or school buses between 1992 and 1998. This includes the following, mostly forgotten legacy from the previous decade that anyone can find mapped out in clickable fashion on the MSNBC Web site (www.MSNBC.com) and other sources:

- May 1, 1992, Olivehust, CA—Eric Houston, 20, killed four people and wounded 10 in an armed siege at his former high school. Houston was angry over a failing grade.

- October 30, 1995, Richmond, VA—Edward Earl Spellman, 18, shot and wounded four students outside their high school.

- February 2, 1996, Moses Lake, WA—Barry Loukaitas, 14, killed his teacher and two male classmates and wounded a girl with an assault rifle. A loner who loved guns, he had previously told friends it would be cool to go on a killing spree like in the Oliver Stone movie *Natural Born Killers*. He was particularly angry at a popular classmate who had called him "a fag." That was the first person he killed.

- July 26, 1996, Los Angeles, CA—High school junior Yohao Albert Rivas, 18, shot and wounded two students in a stairwell on campus.

- February 19, 1997, Bethel, AK—After making multiple threats, Evan Ramsey, 16 fatally gunned down his high school principal and one of his classmates with a 12-gauge shotgun. The motive? He thought it would be "cool."

- October 1, 1997, Pearl, MS—Luke Woodham, 16, stabbed his mother to death, then headed to school with a 30-30 rifle hidden inside a trench coat. He opened fire in the cafeteria, killing his ex-girlfriend and another student, and wounding seven more. He testified that he was under the influence of a devil-worshiping youth gang known as The Kroth that played violent games and conjured up spells against their enemies.

- December 1, 1997, Paducah, KY—Michael Carneal, 14, entered his high school packing a .22 caliber pistol, two shotguns, and two rifles. He headed for a prayer meeting where he used the pistol to shoot eight students, killing three. "It was kind of like I was in a dream," he told the principal, giving that as his only explanation.

- December 15, 1997, Stamps, AR—Joseph "Colt" Todd, 14, was arrested in the sniper shooting of two students outside their high school. The students recovered. Todd said he was tired of being picked on by kids who bullied him and took his money.

- March 24, 1998, Jonesboro, AR—Mitchell Johnson, 13, and Andrew Golden, 11, set off a fire alarm at Westside Middle School and started picking off students and teachers as they poured out of the building. Four female students and a teacher were killed, while one teacher and nine students were injured. The youths gave little insight into their motive, just that they wanted to scare people.

- April 24, 1998, Edinboro, PA—Teacher John Gillette was shot dead at a school dance, allegedly by Andrew Wurst, 14. Two students and another teacher were wounded. Wurst had previously threatened to go on a murder-suicide spree.

- May 19, 1998, Fayetteville, TN—Three days before his graduation, Jacob Davis, an 18-year-old honor student, opened fire in the school parking lot, killing Robert Creson, a classmate who was dating his ex-girlfriend.

- May 21, 1998, Springfield, OR—Kip Kinkel, a 15-year-old freshman, blasted away in the cafeteria, killing two and wounding 22. Kinkel's parents were later found dead in their home. Students reported that Kinkel was obsessed with guns, bombs, and violent television shows. He was angry about being suspended the day before for bringing a gun to school.

- April 20, 1999, Littleton, CO—Eric and Dylan ravaged Columbine High. This one got all the attention, but the school rage continued.

- May 20, 1999, Conyers, GA—T.J. Solomon wounded six peers with a pistol and shotgun at Heritage High School. Solomon's lawyer claims the attack was due to a mental collapse, possibly triggered in part by the drug Ritalin, generally prescribed for psychological disorders.

- November 20, 1999, Deming, NM—Dressed in camouflage, 13-year-old Victor Cordova, Jr. fatally shot a 13-year-old female classmate in the head at their school. Cordova, depressed over the recent death of his mother, and fighting feelings of alienation, had told fellow students, "Watch, I'm going to make history blasting this school."

- December 6, 1999, Fort Gibson, OK—Four students were shot at a middle school in this sheltered farm town 50 miles southeast of Tulsa. A 13-year-old student is suspected.

- February 29, 2000, Mount Morris Township, MI—A 6-year-old girl was fatally shot in her first-grade classroom, allegedly by a 6-year-old boy.

- May 26, 2000, Lake Worth, FL—A seventh-grade teacher was shot to death during the last period on the final day of classes. A student was arrested as he attempted to flee.

- March 5, 2001, Santee, CA—A small, thin freshman who was frequently the butt of jokes told friends all weekend that he was going to shoot up his school, Santana High near San Diego. No one took him seriously, and he later assured them he was just kidding. He wasn't. That Monday, Charles Andy Williams stationed himself inside a bathroom in the quad section of the campus and began firing with a nine shot, .22 caliber handgun, killing two fellow students and injuring 13 teenagers and adults. Witnesses said he wore a big smile as he mowed down those around him in the bathroom and the surrounding courtyard.

- March 7, 2001, Williamsport, PA—A 14-year-old girl attending a Catholic junior high school decided to settle a feud with another girl by firing a gun into the cafeteria ceiling and floor. The bullet apparently ricocheted up and hit the second girl in the shoulder. The shooter, Elizabeth Catherine Bush, then alternated between threatening others, and holding the gun to her own head. A boy, Brent Paucke, 14, heroically talked her into putting down the weapon.

- March 22, 2001—El Cajon, CA—Angry at a Vice Principal over some unspecified grievance, Granite Hills High School senior Jason Hoffman came to class armed with a 12-gauge shotgun and .22-caliber pistol. He crouched in a sniper position and began firing toward the administration building. Three students and a teacher were wounded, and another five suffered minor injuries from flying glass and falling down during the ensuing panic.

As with Columbine, the conservatives blamed liberals, the liberals blamed conservatives, the African-Americans blamed whites, the whites blamed African-Americans, the Christians blamed non-Christians, the non-Christians blamed Christians, religious folks blamed atheists, atheists blamed religious folks, educators blamed Hollywood, Hollywood blamed educators, teachers blamed parents, parents blamed teachers—and nothing was ever resolved. As New Jersey's Bill Bradley, former professional basketball star turned U.S. Senator, lamented in the mid-1990s, "The murderers are younger, the guns more high-powered, and the acts themselves occur more and more randomly." That statement now stands as a chilling omen as to what was to come.

A check with the National Center for Education Statistics reveals that such lawful breakdowns are hardly a surprise. During the 1996-97 school year, there were nearly 4,000 rapes and related sexual batteries reported in American schools. There were almost 11,000 physical attacks and fights that involved a weapon, plus another

190,000 in which the combatants relied on old-fashioned punches and kicks. Round out those statistics with 7,000 robberies, 115,000 thefts, and 98,000 incidents of vandalism, and the picture darkens further.

The U.S. Department of Education reports that 5,724 students were expelled in 1996-97 for bringing a firearm to school, followed by another 3,910 in 1997-98. These figures only include those who were expelled for a full year as Federal Law mandates, not those who were privately scolded and warned.

A 1992 survey conducted by the respected Joseph and Edna Josephson Institute of Ethics and quoted in *Education World* Magazine, found that 33 percent of all high school students admitted stealing merchandise from a store within the previous year, 61 percent admitted cheating on an examination, 83 percent said they lied to their parents, 33 percent were willing to lie on a résumé to get a job, and 16 percent had already done so.

Why has all this immoral, sociopathic madness happened? Kevin Ryan, President of the Center for the Advancement of Ethics and Character at Boston University, offers a hint in an article he wrote for *The American Enterprise*: "From the beginning, character formation has been part and parcel of public education. But by the 1960s our history teachers insisted we had no moral heritage to bequeath to our children. 'Who are we to impose our values on the young?' they asked. And so for the past 30 years our schools have been value-free-zones."

The Character Education Partnership (CEP), a nonpartisan coalition of organizations and individuals dedicated to developing moral character and civic virtue in young people, elaborated on this further in a report published in *U.S. News & World Report*:

"In America, developing good character in young people was an essential part of the educational mission from the colonial period through the first part of the 20th century. Colonial schools were originally established to teach children to read so they could read the Bible and better learn and understand religious principles and values. Through much of U.S. history character development of young people has been closely tied to the moral teachings of dominant religious groups in local communities. Such lessons were transmitted by schools as well as families, communities and religious institutions. This tradition was continued during the 19th century when *McGuffey's Readers* became the most widely used school books through the United States. The readers were full of Biblical stories and other moral lessons. During most of the period since the mid-1950s, the identification of moral education goals and objectives was greatly reduced in curriculum guides and materials produced by state departments of education and many local schools. . . . Furthermore, as the U.S. population became more diverse through immigration, some parents began to object to religious teaching and practices in the public schools that were incompatible with their own beliefs. The Supreme Court began to uphold such complaints on the basis of the First Amendment to the U.S. Constitution which provides in part 'Congress shall make no law respecting the establishment of religion or prohibiting free exercise thereof . . .' Uncertain of what they could and could not legally do, school officials began to shy away from moral education altogether as a way of avoiding controversy and potential litigation. . . . With the focus on moral education somewhat blurred, many schools turned to 'values clarification' which advocated helping students to explore their own moral views, listen to the views of their classmates, and decide for themselves their own moral precepts and systems. This approach, which lacked a moral anchor, has been largely discredited although it still exists in some schools.

". . . The moral climate in many U.S. schools . . . degenerated to the point where poor attitudes and disciplinary problems among significant numbers of students made constructive education activities increasingly difficult. This situation resulted from a convergence of such factors as family breakdown, poverty, loss of community, negative peer pressures, glorification of sex, violence and materialism in the entertainment media, continuing social injustice, the decline of moral values in society as a whole, and the weakening of positive character education in many families and most schools."

Colorado Governor Bill Owen, speaking before the Heritage Foundation as the one-year anniversary of the Columbine shootings approached, made some similar observations regarding what he saw at Columbine during a post-tragedy tour.

"What stuck out in my mind was what movie posters were on the walls. They didn't have *Gone With the Wind*, they had *Natural Born Killers*. They didn't have *Casablanca*, they did have *The Terminator*. They didn't have *The Sound of Music*, but they did have a poster for *Die Hard*. This is what our children are seeing when they go to school. This is what the children of Columbine saw. This is what too many of our children are being taught. Maybe we can't monitor what our children look at every time they access the Internet, (but) . . . we can monitor absolutely what they see when they walk into our classrooms.

". . . Those two killers broke scores of laws, and one more law, or even a dozen laws, wouldn't have changed the hate that resided so deeply in their hearts. . . . Many of us have wanted to blame violent movies and video games and even Internet sites. However, what all these contributing factors boil down to is the fact that our culture is badly in need of repair and healing."

Creators Syndicate columnist Linda Bowles echoes a related view. "Anyone who reads the paper and watches television would have no trouble believing that behavioral problems among children and teenagers are increasing in number and intensity. Anyone who has lived long enough to compare this generation of children with past generations knows that something is terribly wrong."

All through the 1990s, outspoken former Secretary of Education William J. Bennett repeatedly warned the nation about the crisis that was festering in American schools. Among other causes, Bennett blamed the disintegration of character-based education, along with, to steal the title from one of his books, *The Death of Outrage* over ethical and moral issues that would have been greeted with shock and immediate punishment in prior eras. Eighteen months before Columbine, Bennett offered this prophetic statement as part of his written testimony before the Senate Budget Committee's Education Task Force:

"A final point: Often, political leaders talk about education in terms of economic competitiveness. This is appropriate but insufficient. We should also talk about education as a way of conveying America's moral and political principles and nurturing the character of the young. We should speak about education in the context of human excellence, high standards and national greatness. We must demonstrate an understanding of, and a willingness to articulate and defend, the fundamental purpose of education, which is to engage in the architecture of the soul. That is not only the best way to win; it is also the best way to justify the public's trust."

As Bennett and other educators have pointed out, when violence and lack of discipline increase, education itself falters. Bennett has continued to shout warnings to America through his respected Empower America think tank (founded in 1993 by Bennett; Jack Kemp, former Secretary of Housing and Urban Development; Jean

Kirkpatrick, former U.S. Representative to the United Nations; and Vin Weber, former U.S. Representative from Minnesota), and more directly, by making use of Empower America's popular grassroots Internet web page (*www.empower.org*). One of the most illuminating articles found there is Bennett's annotated list of "20 Troubling Facts about American Education." Among the problems Bennett specified:

- American 12th graders rank 19th out of 21 industrialized countries in mathematics achievement and 16th out of 21 nations in science. Advanced physics students rank dead last.

- Since 1983, more than 10 million Americans have reached the 12th grade without having learned to read at a basic level. More than 20 million have reached their senior year unable to do basic math. Almost 25 million have reached 12th grade not knowing the essentials of U.S. history.

- In the same period, more than 6 million Americans dropped out of high school altogether. In 1996, 44 percent of Hispanic immigrants aged 16-24 were not in school and did not hold a diploma.

- In the fourth grade, 77% of children in urban high-poverty schools are reading "below basic" on the National Assessment of Educational Progress (NAEP).

- Average per-pupil spending in U.S. public schools rose 212 percent from 1960 to 1995 in real (i.e., inflation-adjusted) dollars.

- In 1995, nearly 30% of first-time college freshmen enrolled in at least one remedial course and 80% of all public four-year universities offered remedial courses.

- According to U.S. manufacturers, 40% of all 17-year-olds do not have the math skills and 60% lack the reading skills to hold down a production job at a manufacturing company.

- 76% of college professors and 63% of employers believe that a high school diploma is no guarantee that the typical student has learned the basics.

- In 1996, 64% of high school seniors reported doing less than one hour of homework per night.

- 57% of public schools reported moderate to serious discipline problems in the 1996-97 school year.

(For the full list and references, see Addendum I on page 161.)

The reasons, as mentioned, are numerous and subject to acrimonious debate. Yet dig through the reports, testimony, and articles, and one theme keeps popping up. From Bennett again, in an article he wrote in 1995 for *Commentary*:

"The greatest long-term threat to the well-being of our children is the enfeebled condition—in some sector of our society, the near-complete collapse—of our character-forming institutions. In a free society, families, schools and churches have primary responsibility for shaping the moral sensibilities of the young. The influence of these institutions is determinative; when they no longer provide moral instruction or lose their moral authority, there is very little that other auxiliaries—particularly the federal government—can do. . . . There are other signs of cultural decay, particularly of the cultural variety. Television shows make a virtue of promiscuity, adultery, homosexuality, and gratuitous acts of violence. Rap music celebrates the abuse and torture of women. Advertisements are increasingly erotic, even perverse. And many of our most successful and critically acclaimed movies celebrate brutality, casual cruelty and twisted sex. . . . The consequence is that the moral universe we are sending our children into today is more harsh, more vulgar, and more violent than the moral universe most of us grew up in—and they are less equipped to deal with it. We should not flinch from admitting this unsettling truth: we live in a culture which seems dedicated to the corruption of the young, to assuring the loss of their innocence before their time. 'It dawned on me recently,' the anthropologist David Murray has written, 'that we have now become the kind of society that in the 19th Century almost every Christian denomination felt compelled to missionize.' "

More recently, West Virginia Democratic Senator Robert Byrd added his voice to those who believe the educational sky is falling. "The United States has never been more affluent in terms of material wealth and creature comforts, or more impoverished in terms of spiritual well-being. It is the best of times materially. It is the worst of times spiritually. . . . We have seen the Supreme Court rule, again and again, against allowing voluntary prayer in public school, [an] ingrained predisposition against expressions of religious or spiritual beliefs . . . completely contrary to the intent of the founders of this great nation."

Have we reached a point of no return? Is there a solution? Some say that in this age of rocketing technology, where last year's computers and Internet sites are already passé, the solution might very well lie in the past. Consider this from British statesman Edmund Burke, written 200 years ago: "Manners are of more importance than laws. Upon them, in a great measure, the laws depend. The law touches us but here and there, and now and then. Manners are what vex or soothe, corrupt or purify, exalt or debase, barbarize or refine us, by a constant steady, uniform, insensible operation, like that of the air we breathe in. They give their whole form and color to our lives. According to their quality, they aid morals, they supply them, or they totally destroy them."

Could it be that simple? Can some 18th century idealism regarding manners, morals, and character education reverse the plague of violence and decay in America's schools today? And even if educators tried, would America's morally rudderless students embrace a concept so simple, and so archaic, as good manners?

Shockingly, it's already happening. And even more shockingly, in some dramatic and exhilarating cases, it's not coming from the teachers and administrators, but from the students themselves. The "Eric and Dylan" generation most affected by the violence, vandalism, turmoil, spiraling teenage suicide, and plummeting SAT scores is reaching back into Edmund Burke's past and demanding that they be taught how to properly behave. They want to learn how to respect each other, how to act with class and dignity, and how to live their lives based upon a clear set of moral guidelines.

Even before Columbine, this strange, unexpected, but wonderfully inspiring form of "corrective evolution" began germinating from specific points in the midwest. A student-inspired movement toward character education—manners, if you will—has already taken hold there, and it's created such a sensation that it's reverberating across the once politely fruited plains and pulsing out to both coasts.

Brace yourself for a high school story that doesn't involve automatic weapons, pipe bombs, bloody hallways, drugs, coed showers, oral sex clubs, teen pregnancies, AIDS, foul language, tragic suicide, illiterate seniors, or any other headline-grabbing horrors of the late 20th century. Brace yourself for a story about the return to the concept of young people wanting to exhibit traits of dignity, class, and personal character.

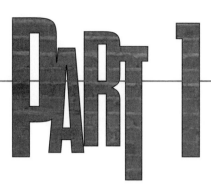

PART 1

FAST TIMES AT MUNDELEIN HIGH AND THE STUDENTS WHO HAD ENOUGH

CHAPTER 1

TROUBLE BREWS
AT AN ILLINOIS
BLACKBOARD JUNGLE

The mid-1990s was a rough time at Mundelein High, a suburban, ranch-styled, tan-and-sandstone school set in a similarly named community about an hour's drive northwest of Chicago. When it came to raising the hackles of teachers and administrators, the classes of '96 and '97 were a particularly rambunctious and competitive bunch. They careened through their four years on the sprawling, 37-acre campus seemingly consumed with outdoing each other in everything from rude assembly shouting contests to an assortment of time-honored school pranks. With each group feeling it needed to top the other, once playful traditions began taking on darker, disquieting tones.

The class of 1996's annual fall Senior Girls Sleepover in the school gym the night before Homecoming 1995 was the first sign of the pending Mundelein meltdown. What began in the early 1960s as a playful, girls-in-rollers, let's go ga-ga over pictures of Elvis type of pajama party had transcended into a much wilder night of 1990s anything goes attitude. Proving they could raise hell just like the boys, the young ladies of Mundelein frolicked through the long evening splattering grease and petroleum jelly into locks and lockers, coating doorknobs with similar slimy substances, shedding intimate apparel in unique places, and dotting the walls with painted handprints.

"When I arrived at school the next morning the courtyard was just trashed," recalls then freshman Brian McSweeney. "There were bras strapped to the windows, condoms wrapped around the pay phones and spray paint everywhere. There was even a Volkswagen Beetle sitting there on the grass. It was a lot of crazy, crazy stuff. I think they even broke a window. I know their behavior was getting worse and worse over the years, but at the time, I thought it was pretty cool. That's high school."

In between the low-level, *Grease*-style hooliganism, the more mature seniors did manage to perform the actual intended purpose of the sleepover and decorated the school for the upcoming festivities, putting up banners and posters, and hanging red-and-white crepe paper to accent the school colors. But they didn't stay up for long. As was also a more recent Mundelein tradition, the rest of the 1,600-strong student body promptly tore down and ripped apart the decorations 10 minutes into the next morning.

The one-two-three punch of greased lockers, painted walls, and trashed adornments was too much for Mundelein Principal John Davis to handle. The normally mellow and easy-going Davis indefinitely suspended the Senior Girls Sleepover, tradition be damned. No sense giving the eager girls of '97 the opportunity to outdo the '96ers' mess.

An overall air of disrespect permeated the halls as the 95-96 school year proceeded. Everyone seemed to be waiting for the next big vandalism shoe to drop. Assemblies became rowdy shout fests, with one class trying to out insult the other. Chants of "freshmen suck!," "juniors suck!," etc., rang out during pep rallies and athletic events. The classes spent more time engaged in uncivil warfare than they did focusing on the common enemy of a rival school. The language overheard in the halls made more than one teacher blanche, while others simply shut their classroom doors, wondering what was happening to the youth of America.

The big shoe—or more specifically, the black, Doc Martin boot that was popular at the time—dropped at the start of the 1996-97 school year. It was another Mundelein tradition that the seniors decorate the school the night before to "welcome" the new freshman and other classes. Over the years, the "decorations" grew into a relatively harmless opportunity to "TP the place"—that is, dress the trees and buildings with Maypole-like streamers of toilet paper. The class of 1997, not wanting to be outdone by the '96 senior girls slumber fiasco, put an extra effort into their TP job. Armed with plastic bottles of ketchup and mustard, they attempted to write insults and slogans on the walls Charles Manson *Helter Skelter*-style. The condiments, however, made for bad writing instruments, so they basically ended up just creating a colossal mess. To make matters worse, the custodial staff members who tried to stop the vandalism were met with obscenities and searing insults to their "lowly" professions.

"A group of us 'nicer' kids started out earlier in the evening doing the normal things, throwing the toilet paper, and spelling out the class names with plastic cups," former cheerleader and pom-pom girl Lisa McSweeney explains. "Then, after we finished, another group came around 3 A.M. and did the wilder stuff. They spray painted the trees and ground, and put shaving cream on the grass, which kills it. That kind of thing. The police were called and one girl was caught and taken in for doing the spray painting."

All of which led to the hot-button homecoming activities less than two months later. Rebuffed in their attempt to resurrect the Senior Girls Sleepover, and given only a single hall to decorate after school, the rowdy senior class of '97 decided to make the homecoming assembly one to remember. They focused their mischief on the method of selecting the Homecoming Queen. It was yet another Mundelein tradition to do this in a way that pumped some drama into the process. Usually, the five leading candidates were brought onstage and handed various boxes or items, one of which would designate the winner. Most often roses were used. The young lady who received the different colored roses—say yellow as opposed to red— was the one the students had voted as their queen. The class of '97, however, figured that was way too boring. Instead, they called the girls on stage, sat each of them in front of a large bucket filled with chocolate pudding, and had them dip their hands into the gooey muck in search of a bright red cherry. The girl getting the cherry—sexual implication no coincidence—was the winner.

A beautiful, All-American blonde name Megan Happ happened to be the lucky, or unlucky, choice that fateful year. A spirited girl from a highly involved family, Megan fished out the prized cherry. Her elation quickly turned to, at the very least, distraction when one of the losers congratulated her by whipping some excess pudding on her face. The assembled students roared with delight, prompting the other three finalists to follow suit. Although many teachers, parents, administrators, and even some students were aghast, it was basically done in good fun. The uproarious event set the tone for an assembly and pep rally that established new decibel levels for the standard "sophomores suck!" type of chants. Humor aside, it was not one of Mundelein's finer moments. And it was about to get decidedly worse.

As was the norm, the *Mundelein Review* was on hand to capture the crowning. An astute photographer, Todd Heisler, flashed photos of the pudding fight. What began as a private bit of one-upsmanship among classes, along with an admittedly novel way of picking a Homecoming Queen, soon erupted into a major community uproar. The *Pioneer Press*, the parent company of the *Mundelein Review* and other area dailies and weeklies, added fuel to the fire by the way they presented the photos. In a section picturing the Homecoming Queens from many of the surrounding high schools, they plucked in Megan Happ's pudding-coated face and "do" right smack in the middle of the perfectly coifed young beauties from the rival schools. To some, the offending photo resembled a Stephen King nightmare come true—a blood-soaked *Carrie* getting set up for ridicule and emotional devastation at what had previously been her happiest moment.

The Mundelein community, suffice it to say, was not amused. Parents burned up the wires calling each other, the teachers, the principal, the superintendent, and the school board. Megan's mother Kelly, a future school board member who happened to be at the assembly and witnessed the frivolity, was particularly incensed.

"I was appalled," she recalled. "It showed a lack of respect and was insulting. I had tears in my eyes as I watched, not just for my daughter, but for the whole school. I immediately spoke to the principal."

Maggie Johnson, a parent and part-time substitute teacher, was also on hand. "I was subbing that day and attended 'The Crowning.' It was so upsetting! The towns around us call us 'Mundeslime' because they're more affluent and think we're low class. I thought, 'Look at us. We're reinforcing that idea. We are sliming our queen! Our finest!' I spoke with a lot of kids afterward and half of them were as disgusted as I was. It was a low moment for Mundelein."

Mary Ann Beatty, who has had four children attend Mundelein, including spirited daughter Blaire of the now infamous class of '97, was no less outraged. "That was way out of the realm of what was appropriate for any kind of homecoming activity. The thing that bothered me is that the event had to be approved by the faculty to begin with. I wouldn't have allowed it, even if it was just searching for the cherry. The whole connotation of the cherry thing was wrong. And it wasn't hard to anticipate that the students would start throwing the pudding. Someone on the faculty should have stopped and said, 'Can we rethink this?' Then, when the newspaper came out, we were appalled all over again. All the others girls looked perfect in their crowns, and there was Mundelein's queen with a face full of pudding!"

Most of the students, naturally, weren't so alarmed as their parents. This includes Megan's brother, Branden, an underclassman in the audience that day. Tossing out the suspicion that a young male might actually enjoy seeing his older sister get splattered with pudding in front of the whole school, Branden offers a level-headed assessment. "I didn't think it was that big of a deal. It was pretty funny at the time. They do things like that every year. My mom got really mad, though."

Blaire Beatty doesn't share her mother's alarmist views either. To the contrary: "I thought it was great! I love seeing people get all messy. It was especially fun to see the normally 'prim and proper' homecoming queen–types get messed up. It wasn't that big a deal. Everybody was making a big stink about it, especially after the picture hit the newspaper, but I thought that was funny as well. We did something different. You don't need to do the roses and candlelight music thing every year. So, we didn't look that great in the newspaper. So? You can't take life too seriously."

Blaire, a cross-country runner who went on to attend Syracuse University's drama school, noted that the stunt had indeed been approved by the student council faculty advisor. She also remembers an observation she made at the time that puts to rest any doubt regarding the alleged spontaneity of the pudding fight. The keen-eyed actress notes that a tarp had been placed on the floor of the stage prior to the five beauties taking their seats.

"There was no punishment or administrative retaliation immediately afterward," Blaire recalls, referring to the post-newspaper community uproar. "And Megan took it well. She saw the fun."

Lisa McSweeney agrees—to a point. "They had to reach deep into the bucket to get the cherry, so their arms were already coated. When they hugged Megan, it just kind of rubbed off at first. I think one of the girls was from a different clique, the soccer/band group, and she might have been a bit disappointed that she didn't win. She *'may'* have rubbed in the pudding a little too enthusiastically. The other girls were Megan's friends, so that was okay. But that was a bad picture in the newspaper. No way around that. I wouldn't have been too thrilled if it happened to me."

Megan, a journalism student who went on to attend Northwestern University, expresses mixed feelings about the incident to this day.

"High school was a long time ago. There were some great times, and there were some not-so-great times as well. That's high school— young kids learning how to deal with such made-up things as 'popularity' and 'homecoming queen.' . . . Yes, my class was rather free-spirited during our senior year. We were no worse or better than any class to go before or after it, but we just seemed to get caught. Call it bad luck or stupidity or both; we were just a bunch of young people looking for a good time and out to impress the other people in our school. I guess it worked if people are still talking about us now!" she observes with whimsy before getting serious again. "I haven't exactly received a warm welcome in that school after homecoming. Yes, another girl was jealous that I had won this stupid crown and smeared my face with the pudding that we had to dig through in front of the school. I guess to the faculty and staff it must have represented something much worse than it was. Everyone *tried* to forget about it."

But no one forgot. Although Megan disavows any connection between "this stupid incident that most people don't even remember" and the extraordinary, wide-ranging, reverse-revolution that followed, virtually everyone else—from students to parents to teachers, administrators, and staff—see it differently. Megan's unique crowning almost instantly planted the seeds of an inspirational grassroots movement that would not only alter the course of Mundelein High, but of schools from one end of America to the other.

Part of the reason can be attributed to the fascinating group dynamic that comes into play among teenagers attending schools with distinct, almost segregated, class divisions. More than anything, each class wants to establish its own identity. While the classes of '96 and '97 at Mundelein High in Illinois tried to accomplish this by topping each other's rowdiness and pranks, the underclassmen, who endured the squabbling for three long, chaotic years, felt that they'd had enough. While most laughed and enjoyed the spirit of the pudding fight at the time, deep inside they were feeling the same uneasiness that had swept over the parents, teachers, and administrators. Where was this kind of thing heading, and what would they be expected to do the following year to top it? Should they even try?

In the days following the publication of Megan's photo, the juniors became more and more disenchanted. Greased locks, shaving cream on doorknobs, mustard on the walls, ripped-up decorations, pip-squeak freshmen slammed into lockers, sophomores terrorized in the bathrooms, chants of "Freshmen Suck!" and a Homecoming Queen who resembled the horror book character Carrie just wasn't cracking them up like it used to. After being the butt of such indignities themselves, the class of '98, to their credit, was in no mood to reciprocate when it came their turn to be on top of the heap. Groups of juniors began meeting in the halls, outside classrooms, during lunch, and before and after school to express their dismay over what was happening inside their school. An idea began to formulate, then spread, that they should reverse course and pull in the reins on all the immature pranks and posturing before it really got out of hand. Instead of trying to top the childish classes of '96 and '97, they were going to express their individuality by doing an about-face. They would return the school's storied traditions to their original, vandalism-free, pure and wholesome state, and behave with dignity and class.

It was a shockingly novel concept, one that, despite their good intentions, wasn't going to be easy. Complicating matters was the continued presence of those wild and crazy seniors. Learning little from the tremendous community-wide flap caused by the "pudding incident," the class of '97 had one more joke up its collective sleeves. Senior Ditch Day was their last hurrah, and they hurrahed to the

max. An underaged beer blast at a house near the school—no surprise in high school communities—got so out of hand with heavy
drinking and loud music that the overworked Mundelein Men in
Blue had to be called out to the scene. More than a dozen slow-
footed students—many of them members of the school's prestigious
National Honor Society—were corralled by the cops. Parents and
administrators were ushered in to sort out the latest frolic and hand
down various forms of private and official punishments.

"There were just some wild kids in our class," Lisa McSweeney
sighs, stressing that her parents refused to let her skip school that
day. "Yeah, some of the first-day-of-school spray painting and year-
end drinking got out of hand, but we weren't the first class that did
those kinds of things. We just kept getting caught. We were kind of
stupid about it. Being rowdy and dumb is a bad combination."

That was certainly a sentiment the Mundelein juniors shared, and
they had no intention of following in their predecessors' "rowdy and
dumb" shoes.

"The thing that triggered our being fed up was what happened at
homecoming that year and in previous years" says Bill Zasadil, '98,
Mundelein's standout football quarterback. "They were defacing the
school rather than decorating it. It was more of a revolt than a celebration. They even insulted the principal by writing 'John Davis
sucks' in chalk across the parking lot. Homecoming wasn't the place
for that kind of thing.

"A second problem we had was that Mundelein has a large Hispanic population, and there was a real gap bringing these kids in
socially with the rest of the school. Some didn't speak English very
well, and there was a total lack of communication between them and
the American students. They hung around together in packs, and
there was lots of testosterone and tension in the halls. At breakfast
one morning, we were sitting down having muffins, and all of a
sudden a chair flies toward us and smacks down on the table, causing a shower of milk and muffins and cookies. Apparently, someone
in our group said something to someone in their group, dissed somebody, or exchanged a dirty look, who knows, but that's all it took.
The next thing I knew there was a full-scale brawl going on.

"Another time, there was this Mexican kid—a gang member—who
had his locker next to the one I shared with another student. He would
always keep his door wide open and pushed back so we couldn't

get into our locker. I let it go for a while, but one day the guy I shared the locker with, a smaller underclassman, moved this kid's door out of the way so he could get to his books. The guy took it as an affront and wanted to fight over it. I stepped between them and he came after me. I shoved him in the locker and kept banging him with the door until he gave in. It bothered me afterward because I'm not the type to go off like that. I had known most of these Mexican guys since middle school, and got along with them. But the tension at Mundelein was growing, and it was starting to get to me as well. That guy's obvious confrontational behavior pushed me too far."

From Zasadil's perspective, the school was boiling over from many different pots. He expected to be attacked on the football field by opposing players, not in the hallways by fellow students. He expected a rival school to try to tear down their homecoming decorations, not his own classmates.

"We lost the homecoming game that year, then there was the picture in the paper of our queen just totally wrecked with pudding. That Monday, I was hanging around outside French 301 with Dave Nellans, Brian Spangle, Jennifer Bouteille, and some others and we were talking about how the seniors weren't representing the school well and how we were embarrassed by their actions. The seniors had an overall attitude that they didn't care about anything but partying. They were selfish and without class. We also talked about how our high school already had a reputation of being low class because we were in a blue-collar neighborhood. We were mostly bright kids with good, hardworking parents. We were not Jerry Springer-type people who lived in trailers. We wanted to get rid of that image we'd been stuck with and the seniors weren't helping."

As the kids were talking, Karen Royer, the French 301 teacher, was listening intently from inside the classroom. She sensed an opportunity. "Ms. Royer basically opened up her French class and gave us the floor to continue what we were saying," Zasadil recalls. "She allowed us to express our opinions about what we thought needed to be changed, and the events that had happened that we found so distasteful. She let us keep talking about it after that class as well. For pretty much the whole semester that was our main discussion in French class. We learned a little French, but we worked more on the problems surrounding the school. I think she was great for allowing us to do that.

"The discussions sparked the development of what we wanted to do the following year when we were seniors. We started identifying roles, choosing leaders, and carrying out various tasks aimed at getting things done. One of the first things we did was pass a petition around to see if other students agreed with us that there needed to be dramatic behavior changes. I went out with it myself, as did the others from Ms. Royer's class. Most of the students were pretty positive about it. There were some who scoffed and wouldn't sign. There are always students who just want to be rowdy. At that age, kids have a lot to figure out, like who we are, what we want to be, what we want to stand for. Others who were skeptical just wanted to be assured that it would really work, that they could expect real changes for their efforts. What I heard was 'How can we get the administration to listen?' They didn't want to get excited about something, only to be shut down. The overall climate was that everybody wanted the place to be stable and supportive, not anarchistic."

Zasadil and his buddies collected between 600 and 700 signatures, close to half of the 1,500 underclassmen. From there, it was back to French class to brainstorm some more. That's where the idea of behavior education was conceived. "It was our group's suggestion to have actual classes on these character issues. We didn't want what was happening among us to be just a flash in the pan, here today, gone tomorrow. The only way to prevent that was to establish a class period that provided a forum for students to discuss ways to better the school and themselves, and give them a voice in what was happening at school. And it couldn't be just once a semester or so. It had to be more often, like once a week.

"After that, we had open forums in the auditorium to see what the rest of the students thought. We passed around flyers and invited everyone to 'tell us what you don't like about our school.' To our surprise, there was a great show of people, about a hundred for each of the three meetings. You could feel the groundswell of support building. People all over the school started talking about it."

Everybody, it seems, but the seniors.

"They were out of it," Zasadil, now a University of Wisconsin finance major, says with a laugh. "I never heard anything from them about it. They never said a word even when the rest of the school was talking and going to the meetings. They went their way, drinking and partying. By mid-year, we juniors had pretty much taken the school over anyway. There was a tradition that the seniors sat in a certain section during basketball games and did various creative things to support the team. There was hardly anybody there, so we juniors took over that section, wore hard hats with the players' names, and got the spirit back up. The seniors never even challenged us about it either."

One of Zasadil's cohorts, Jennifer Bouteille (Boo-tay), was a spunky freshman who found herself swept up in junior tide due to a familiar bit of grade-point trickery. Her parents had emigrated from France, and she spoke the language fluently. Like fellow bilingual students since the dawn of time, Jennifer sandbagged the language class of her family heritage for an easy "A." Her fluency, and "a desire to brush up on my French writing" (wink, wink), enabled her to jump right into the third-year level 301 class with all the juniors. (To her credit, Bouteille took two years of Spanish as well.) It was a fateful placement, as she became the only Mundelein freshman to be at ground zero of the Character Education movement. That meant she would have three years of school left to see where, if anywhere, it was heading.

"We juniors were two-thirds of the way through when it started, and only had one year to see where it went," Zasadil acknowledges. "Jennifer had basically her whole high school experience ahead of her, so it was great that she was there with us from the beginning. She could take it all the way."

Like the juniors who adopted her, the feisty, lighthaired, French soccer player started off her high school career by recoiling at what she was seeing happening around her. "The tacky homecoming 'decorations,' then other students ripping them down, it was so ridiculous," she recalls. "It wasn't spirit, it was hatred! It was my first homecoming so I really didn't know what to expect when things got crazy, but I could tell the juniors were upset. We were talking about it before French class, then Mr. Davis came on the school's television and spoke about how horrible he thought it was, so that kind of reiterated what we had been saying. We continued to talk about how we needed to get the ball rolling to do something about it. We decided that the students had to lead this or it would fail. The administration and teachers could be involved, but we had to take the lead because we felt it would be more effective coming from students rather than teachers. The students would listen more to their peers on these behavior issues."

Bouteille certainly took the idea to heart. Like Zasadil, she spent days pigeonholing every student in sight to sign that initial petition, which, in essence, was a demand that the administration give the students the opportunity to right their own ship.

"I think I got the most signatures. I didn't eat lunch for three days. I went to various after-school clubs, approached people in the halls before and after classes, during sports practices, I was just everywhere. My main focus was to get everybody, not just jocks and cliques but everybody—the Latins, Goths (self-exiled outcasts who dressed in black), underclassmen, upperclassmen. I approached everybody and said, 'Do you like what's been happening around here? Is this how you want the school to be?' Some were a bit hesitant to sign. They thought that by signing they were committing themselves to some work or effort. 'What's this for?' they'd asked. 'I don't want to get involved.' But I'd explain it to them and they'd sign. Everybody signed. I was pretty aggressive about it."

She was also just plain pretty, which always helps, and she was culturally diverse as well. "I lived in a Hispanic neighborhood, so I'd been with that crowd on the bus since eighth grade. I got them to sign as well. They were happy to be included!"

Despite her unbridled enthusiasm, Bouteille admits she did have her doubts about how the entire student body would actually react when it came time for them to step forward.

"Before the open forums, we handed out these little flyers to get people to come. That was a big step. I mean, I was worried that no one would show. The flyers were being tossed on the ground and stuffed in the garbage. It was really disheartening. Ms. Royer said, 'Don't worry, if they see them on the ground, they'll get the message.' On the day of the first meeting, I was really nervous. I wasn't expecting very many people. Well, when they started piling in, I couldn't believe it! There were so many people! That really gave us a boost. Then during the meeting, everybody was vocal. They wanted to change! And every group was there from the jocks to the Goths. I went to all three of the open forums and was continually amazed at the showing. Many people came back and brought their friends. Even the teachers came. This thing was really building!

"Afterward, we sent a letter to the superintendent explaining what we were doing, the support we were getting, and what we wanted to do. He came to one of our meetings and saw how serious and organized we were. He was impressed."

So were a lot of others. As the effort spread, more and more students from outside Ms. Royer's class were brought into the group. Junior Julie Waskey, a straight-laced, future teacher, jumped on board when she was approached.

"The senior class before us was just horrible," Waskey confirms. "They did a lot of bad stuff. I'm not into smearing the halls with shaving cream and greasing locks and pranks like that. They had beer parties and kept getting caught by the police. They'd go to someone's house for lunch and drink, then come back to school drunk. One time they got busted right during lunch! The parents were called in and everything.

"I don't agree with drinking at all, much less in the middle of the school day. What idiots! I can't believe they were coming to class drunk. People kind of laughed. They thought it was funny. I don't recall the teachers making note or doing anything. Maybe they didn't notice, but it was hard not to. We all noticed.

"Our class just didn't like that kind of stuff," Waskey continues. "We couldn't believe how they'd trash our school. School was like our home, basically. We were there every day. Why trash where you live?"

Throughout the previous years, as the classes of '96 and '97 began altering the school's annual traditions in mischievous ways, Principal John Davis started suspending various events and tempering others. Aside from losing the sleepover, there were restrictions placed on when, where, and how the school could be decorated for homecoming and other annual events; severe limitations on what they could and couldn't do to celebrate the beginning and ending of the school year; and, to top it off, they were no longer allowed to eat lunch off campus so often.

"As these things were taken away, we'd go to Mr. Davis all the time and said, 'Why are you taking stuff from us because of them?' Waskey continues. " 'That's not fair.' He would respond that he realized that, which is why he allowed the character education program to start with us. That was good, I guess, but we still wanted our traditions back. The administration kept praising us and making us look like the 'glowing' class, while at the same time, they kept taking our stuff from us. Davis would just keep saying, 'I know there are traditions but sometimes traditions need to change.' I felt he should have trusted us more. When we decorated, we did clever and cutesy things, nothing harmful. We made the place look good.

"I don't know why our two classes were so different. The seniors of '97 were isolated among themselves. We had very little to do with them. We interacted much more with the classes under us. I think that was part of the problem. Personally, I was never into the beer blast scene."

Waskey, now a Western Illinois education student, said that like many students, she jumped on a moving train and was not aware of the birth of the character movement in Ms. Royer's French class.

"I heard some talk about it early on but it was kind of faint. Then, as the year progressed, it built. I wanted to be part of it. I like being involved in positive things. I thought it would be beneficial, and the people stepping forward were all my friends. I knew nothing could happen while the class of '97 was still around. That would have been a disaster. They would have just rejected it and laughed it off.

"The plan was to launch the program at the beginning of our senior year. We were against what had happened before us, and we really wanted to do this. That's why the momentum built. Another important factor was that our class was close to the faculty. Some of us thought of the teachers as friends."

Once the juniors had their ideas in place, they started testing the waters by seeing if the sophomores were interested in joining them. Shane Chareonshump, a popular, six-foot-one Thai athlete, was one of the first to be recruited.

"This junior, Billy Zasidal, approached me about going to a meeting they were holding to discuss what we could do to improve the school. I said, 'Yeah, sure. I'll go.' I wasn't happy with the overall aura of the place. We were picked on pretty bad the year before as freshmen. I remember being slammed into lockers at least four times, and I'm pretty big. There was just too much division, disrespect, and competition among classes. There was a good camaraderie within the classes themselves, but nothing that brought us all together. And it wasn't classy having your homecoming queen covered in pudding on the front page of the newspaper. It made our school look bad. So if these juniors wanted to change things, I was all for it.

"What I liked was that there were few or no teachers, and no administrators, at those first meetings. It was just we students working this out among ourselves, trying to turn this thing around. We talked about showing more spirit and getting more kids involved with the school. It was really nice the way it developed."

By late spring, the juniors' plotting began to pique the curiosity of a number of the distracted and troublesome seniors. By then, Mundelein's elder class had one foot out the door, eagerly looking forward to a brave new world beyond high school. That made them even less inclined than before to bother with altering their behavior. Still, there was some kind of weird movement afoot, and a few were taking notice.

"We started hearing some rumblings toward the end of the year that the juniors were going to do this 'character' thing," Blaire Beatty remembers. "They never really got us involved because we were on our way out, and they probably viewed us as the problem to begin with. My reaction was that I was going to Syracuse University and I could care less," she joked. "Truthfully, I heard my younger brother talk about it, and I distinctly remember the junior leaders at a National Honor Society meeting saying, 'We are going to be better seniors.' That's the normal thing to say, but not from a behavioral standpoint! Usually they mean they are going to be better at being rowdy. It was intriguing, but I was pessimistic about it. It sounded like a great thing in concept, and the less adults involved the better, so that aspect was encouraging. But overall it seemed to be a reach. If the effort truly was coming from the students themselves, I felt it did have a better chance of working. I had to give them that."

Blaire suspects that the reason the behavior of her class continued to disintegrate was a reaction to the administration's "heavy-handed" tactics of trying to discipline them by tightening up the rules, and suspending their long-standing traditions and privileges. "The discipline was coming down hard and we rebelled," she says. "Plus, our class was the first hit with the new 'block scheduling' concept of changing to fewer, longer classes during the school day, and that was disorienting for everybody. We were used to a lot of shorter classes with more breaks in between, and the longer blocks were tiring. Then, the administration decided not to name a valedictorian and a salutatorian because they didn't want to elevate one student over another and make anybody 'feel bad,' which I thought was pretty dumb. So instead of having a valedictorian speak at the graduation ceremony, we had to vote on it. We ended up voting for the girl who would have been our valedictorian. Who'd have thunk it, huh? So all those changes really weighed on us and caused some of the chaos and confusion."

With those excuses offered, Blaire admits her class could have been a wee bit more respectful. She was also "voted" to speak (she probably would have been the salutatorian) at graduation and recalls tackling the notorious behavioral problem head on. "I noted that we didn't have to go on to be such 'slackers.' We could actually go and accomplish something with our lives."

Blair's classmate, Lisa McSweeney, who went on to become an elementary education student at Illinois State, adds that the juniors' character education hoopla was rubbed in the seniors' faces at their school's final assembly. "Mr. Davis made a point of saying that the school was going in that direction; that the juniors didn't want the school to be bad anymore. I was really embarrassed because not all of us had misbehaved. But I graduated two days later so I didn't have to deal with it."

Yet, like Beatty and others with younger siblings still at Mundelein, McSweeney was interested in seeing what would develop at her alma mater. Beatty, the daughter of a high school teacher, paid particular attention. "As for the juniors and these bold new ideals of theirs, it was going to take a lot of work to get something like that started, even if it was student inspired. Then again, maybe since our class was so 'bad,'" she adds with bemusement, "it was an incentive for the next class to shape up. That's good in theory. But in practice, I wasn't so sure."

A good effort for sure, but as Beatty noted, one that was going to take a lot of work. Try as they might, the incoming seniors weren't going to be able to make these changes on their own. For their plan to really take hold, they needed help. They needed the support of their teachers.

CHAPTER 2

TEACHERS TO THE RESCUE

Mundelein French teacher Karen Royer is the kind of upbeat, spirited, and highly enthusiastic educator who administrators seek, parents admire, and students adore. Even though the popular, Green Bay, Wisconsin native taught a difficult elective, her classrooms were always filled. Royer's engaging, caring personality and encouraging teaching style had transformed what is usually an unpleasant high school language requirement into the pulse of the entire school. If something exciting or controversial was in the wind, public or private, the issue invariably landed on Ms. Royer's desk.

Yet, despite her obvious talent, cheerful countenance and optimistic viewpoint, Royer wasn't exactly leaping out of bed each morning to rush eagerly to her noble calling of broadening the linguistic horizons of America's youth. Like so many of her peers, the University of Wisconsin graduate shared the concern that the student body was starting to get out of hand.

Putting things in perspective, the situation at Mundelein High was still far removed from the intercity war zones that double as schools in the massive city of Chicago a short drive away. Even so, everything is relative. The suburban, mostly white, middle-class Mundelein students of the 1990s were doing their part to dim the enthusiasm of their teachers.

"I was shocked when I attended my first pep rally and heard the other classes screaming, 'Freshmen suck!' and that kind of thing," Royer recalls. "It seemed as if the students had no idea that a pep rally was supposed to be an opportunity to cheer on their athletic teams. But that was just one of many things the students were doing that was truly unacceptable. The cafeteria was trashed every day after lunch. The main bathrooms were thick with cigarette smoke and the walls were covered with graffiti; many students walked across campus to more isolated bathrooms rather than entering them. And, like the pep rallies, the homecoming activities seemed to be nothing more than a chance to exhibit embarrassing behavior. The girls would stay up all night to decorate the school and then the next morning the other students would come and rip everything down."

Count Royer among those who viewed homecoming '96 as the breaking point. "I was at nearby Lake Forest High School attending their homecoming ceremonies because my son was on the court. To choose the queen, he walked up and down a line of finalists holding the crown, then he placed it on the winner's head. During that whole assembly, I felt that the students had an enormous pride in their school and campus. They had bought into the concept that the students 'owned their school.' When I returned to Mundelein I heard all about the contrasting way we had chosen our queen. The cherry thing was vulgar and suggestive, and the subsequent pudding fight got out of hand. I'm glad I wasn't there to witness it."

Thanks to the follow-up newspaper photos, Royer was far from alone in her feelings. What was unusual, however, was the ages of some of those who shared her point of view.

"Often, the more active students and student leaders would gather outside my classroom and discuss various current events. Sometimes I'd just listen. Once in a while, I'd join in. On this particular morning, the Monday after homecoming, I heard a group of juniors talking about how disgusted they were with what had happened at homecoming, and with the student body as a whole. That certainly made my ears wiggle."

To her credit, Royer decided to seize the opportunity. She scrapped her entire lesson plan that day and continued the hallway conversation inside.

"We spent the entire 90-minute class talking about what was wrong with Mundelein. Everyone saw the pudding incident as the straw that broke the camel's back. One student after another expressed how sick and tired they were of stupid senior stunts, the rampant smoking, graffiti, and trash in the bathrooms, and the cafeteria litter. What impressed me was that they also addressed the air of disrespect the students were displaying toward the faculty, and the similar disrespect the faculty was in turn showing toward the students. I had to admit they were right on both ends. Although we adults are supposed to set the examples, after years of receiving verbal abuse and disrespect, we started treating the students the way we were being treated.

"When the bell rang, I couldn't help but feel exhilarated and thrilled by what I'd just experienced. This was a group of young people who wanted to rekindle the basic concept of values! Imagine that?"

After identifying the source of all the problems, mostly the knuckleheads populating the classes of '96 and '97, Royer continued to use her class as a forum to embrace this embryonic movement. "We decided to circulate a petition to see if the school in general felt the same way as this small gathering of fed-up juniors. A group of nine students, mostly those from that original French class, took the initiative to pass the petitions around the school."

Aside from the previously mentioned Bill Zasadil, Jennifer Bouteille, Brian Spangle, and David Nellans, Royer identified the remaining trailblazers as Stephanie Grumbeck, Angela Hebert, Christopher Smith, and Emily Spear—plus Samantha Kelley, a rare, reverse renegade from the senior class.

"I'm going from memory, but the petition was short and to the point," Royer explains. "Something like: 'We the undersigned feel that there are certain changes in terms of behavior that we have noticed in our school (as exemplified by Homecoming) that need to be addressed. If you agree, sign.' Well, we were all overwhelmed by the response. They returned with a great number of signatures!"

Armed with the healthy stack of petitions, Royer felt it was time to bring the issue before the school's administration, a decision that took no small amount of courage and gumption. Regardless of her good intentions, the French teacher suspected that taking the student demands to the administration would, at best, be greeted cooly because such "bottomsup" movements are always risky. Schools in general, and administrators in particular, are usually locked into the "top-down" philosophy of education. The rule of thumb is that administrators generate concepts and curriculum, teachers apply them, and the students keep their mouths shut and literally go with the program. Anything to the contrary is usually met with a swift veto. And this goes double for behavioral issues.

Rather than face a rebuff and quash their grassroots effort before it started, Royer and gang decided to recruit a teacher/administrator hybrid who could carry some weight in the principal's office. They targeted a man who was no stranger to the twin concepts of discipline and reversing the field—Mundelein High Mustangs football coach John Ahlgrim. Fortunately, it didn't take much to convince Coach Ahlgrim to toss his helmet into the ring.

"Coach was supervising an after-school 'Diversity Club' that was about building respect along racial and social lines. So his ideas were similar to ours," student Jennifer Bouteille explains. "So we said, 'Come on, help us out.' And he said, 'Okay!'"

Ahlgrim, a Notre Dame graduate who doubled as a math teacher and Dean of Students, wasn't sure who initially approached him, but mentioned Bouteille's name first. "This came from the kids. Karen Royer's kids, Bouteille, and two of my players, Bill Zasadil and Luke Hajzl. Luke was a great leader, and Bill was our quarterback. (I remember Jennifer because she's been around the school more recently.) I was encouraged from the beginning because to pull something off like this, you need kids who have leadership instincts. Those three were natural leaders in and of themselves, and they were showing that every day.

"Another reason I came aboard at that early stage was because our principal, John Davis, thought it would help if the students had a legitimate tie-in with the school. As dean and coach, I have contact with a wide circle of kids. After the first few student/teacher meetings, I could see the potential and volunteered to do more. Karen was suited to developing the issues and program, while my strength involved logistics and getting the message out. I was able to get input from all types of student groups, which was important because we needed to represent this as coming from the entire student body."

Royer agrees with Ahlgrim's assessment of their complementary abilities. "I was determined, but I don't know if I could have done it alone. Coach Ahlgrim's support was vital. My master's and strength is in curriculum development, which would come later. Ahlgrim, in his position as dean and coach, could gain access to the overall student body in a quicker fashion."

Royer and Ahlgrim supported the students' decision to ask the administration to give the green light to a series of open forums designed to expand the circle of interest and input. To their pleasant surprise, the administration not only approved, but did so without tying their hands with oppressive guidelines, or saddling them with excessive warnings as to what topics were taboo.

Three meetings were promptly scheduled to allow students, teachers, and staff members to easily fit at least one session into their busy day. They had the option of dropping in before or after school, or during lunch. When D-Day arrived, even the most optimistic, original founder couldn't have anticipated the reaction. More than 100 people showed up for each session. What began as a gripe session outside a French class had stampeded into a nifty little social movement.

The forums became large-scale versions of Royer's first exhilarating French class discussion. All, from shop teachers to chess club members to custodians, were allowed to air their beefs about what was happening at Mundelein. Interestingly enough, the Mundelein masses focused upon the same problems the French class had specified that first day—seniors trashing the campus and how the upperclassmen were turning honored traditions into opportunities to misbehave and vandalize. They also brought up the lack of mutual respect among teachers, students, and staff.

Ahlgrim remembers being blown away by the response. "That's what made us realize, 'Holy Cow, there is something here!' It gave everybody a boost. We began investigating ways to actually get this done. There were a million things to do, and the first was to identify workable goals."

Royer was thinking the same thing, only she wanted to make doubly sure the teachers and administrators didn't just sweep in and take over. "What was so different with this, what made it so attractive from the student perspective, is that it was truly a grassroots idea started by the students. That can't be stressed enough. Anything remotely like it at other schools came from the top down. The goal at those institutions was for the administration to gain control by making rules that forced the students to behave inside the confines of the building. This movement of ours at Mundelein was so much more than that. The students were going to change their behavior themselves, and in turn, the administration was going to regain control as a fringe benefit. Instead of becoming an authoritarian institution like most schools, we were going to become a 'self-reflective' school, meaning that we would determine ourselves who we were as a community, where we were going, and how we were going to get there. The students would determine this, not by following some adult-ordered set of guidelines, but by taking a long and hard look at themselves. This is what packed those meetings."

In essence, the same student-inspired aspect that made the plan such a shaky venture to present to the administration had now become its greatest strength. "We came away from those wonderfully encouraging meetings having accomplished two major objectives," Royer notes. "We not only defined the problem, we narrowed our concerns into three simple goals."

In keeping with popular educational lore, the group developed its own "three Rs" to counter the much quoted concept of "reading, 'riting, and 'rithmatic." Only their Rs didn't involve a painful bending of the language.

"Our tenets were based on the concept of 'respect,'" Royer outlines. "Respect for self and others. Respect for how we communicate. Respect for our school environment."

In retrospect, they might have been wise to add a fourth "R"— "Respect for our detractors." Although the majority of the faculty members allowed themselves to be swept up with the emotional tide, there was indeed some solid opposition. Pumped with youthful energy, the students shrugged and figured they'd simply steamroll any pesky naysayers. After all, they were trying to be good! Who could stand in the way of that? The more mature Royer knew better. Vocal pockets of faculty detractors, however small, were a bigger concern than the students could imagine. Royer feared that, as with any controversial "little-people" moment, a few well-placed obstacles could derail the most high-powered train, especially a runaway one.

"In all group dynamics, you're going to encounter those who are unwilling to make the necessary commitment," Royer explains. "This was going to take an effort to implement, and some teachers didn't feel they should be expected to make such an effort on top of everything else they had to do. Others weren't comfortable with the student-run aspect that was developing. The faculty would be asked to sit back and act as facilitators while the students took control of the program. This was difficult for some teachers to conceive. It's hard for a teacher to defer to the kids. It's understandable that some would have strong reservations about whether it would work."

Soccer coach Dave Ekstrom remembers the early rumblings among the faculty. "I was supportive of what they were trying to accomplish. Most teachers were. However, it was met with some hesitancy because it was viewed as one more thing we had to do. Teachers are busy enough already. We don't need more things to do."

To temper the smoldering opposition, Royer and gang came up with yet another novel concept. The students were sent out in groups of three to personally meet with various gatherings of teachers. In a sense, they were dispatched to sell the concept. Accepting the challenge, they stood before the skeptical, first-line educators and explained what they wanted to accomplish. As an added touch, they looked their teachers in the eye and with no small dramatic flourish, asked 'Will you help us?'"

"What teacher can say 'no' to that?" Royer laughs. "After those meetings, the opposition was tempered considerably."

Bouteille, the spunky freshman who muscled half the student body into signing the petitions, was naturally among those chosen to put the finger on the faculty. "I went with Billy Zasadil and some others to speak with the teachers in little groups. We told them we needed everyone's support. They thought it was some kind of student rebellion thing, so we had to convince them otherwise. Some were like 'yeah, yeah' but you could see that in the back of their heads they were skeptical. It was a lukewarm support at best. They didn't believe we could pull it off."

The detractors underestimated the enthusiasm, widespread student support, and determination of Royer, Ahlgrim, Bouteille, and crew. Plus, the students were further pumped by the clever way they managed to overcome those initial faculty roadblocks. As the turbulent school year of 1996-97 stumbled to a messy, beer-blast-busted end, however, some of the wind was taken out of their sails. For all the rah-rah, what they didn't have was that proverbial precise plan of operation, complete with the footnotes, precedents, and stilted educational phrasing, that is so vital when making a pitch before stodgy educators. Mundelein's suits had given the okay to hold a few relatively harmless, off-hours gripe sessions, but they stopped well short of actually allowing this upstart student movement to invade the sacred and highly regulated confines of the regular school day. To the suits, this was simply a hazy, nonspecific, student-designed concept involving "some kind of character education." Any administrator with a grain of ambition knew better than to bet his career on a hazy, nonspecific, student-designed concept of anything. The teachers and students still had a long way to go before their sugarplum vision of a bold, new G-rated campus environment would do anything other than fizzle out and die over the long, hot, indifferent summer.

CHAPTER 3

WILL THE PRINCIPAL
AND SUPERINTENDENT
"GET IT"?

It had been a rough couple of years for Mundelein High Principal John Davis. The well-respected, former football quarterback at Wisconsin's Carroll College had spent 33 years battling in the academic trenches. The sunset was coming, the textbooks were on their final chapters, and he was looking forward to easing into a peaceful retirement. The last thing he needed was one final generation of wild children painfully passing through his building like a giant porcupine being slowly digested by a snake.

Davis had spent his entire career at Mundelein content to rise through the academic ranks when opportunities became available. He climbed from social studies teacher to Dean of Students, Student Activities Director, Building Manager, and, finally, Principal. A hands-on type deeply involved with the students, he coached football, track, and basketball, and even spent a hectic stint corralling the school's at-risk students in a discipline-challenged, energy-draining alternative program reminiscent of the Sweat Hogs made famous by John

Travolta in the memorable 70s-era television sitcom *Welcome Back Kotter.*

Davis was thus no stranger to virtually anything, good or bad, that could break out inside the unique ecosystem of an American high school. He had already survived the massive student rebellions of the late 1960s and early 1970s when social changes were occurring at warp speed. Back then, students were willing to fight to the death over the seminal issues of long hair, miniskirts, bell-bottoms, love beads, going braless, antiwar protests, acid rock, and other Flower Children and Mod Hipster entitlements. Those were the days when anybody over 30 was viewed as the enemy, and teachers and administrators were the over 30s most immediately in the students' crosshairs.

The aimless *Less Than Zero* mind-set of the 1980s was no picnic for educators either. Drugs became an increasing problem, and the lifeless, ambivalent slacker was the flipside of the activist hippies. Trying to pump some knowledge and ambition into that wandering generation helped put the gray in the hair of thousands of administrators.

The 1990s calmed down in the early part of the decade and things began to even out. Then came the disturbing rash of shocking school shootings and mass murders breaking out from isolated pockets. To Davis's relief, Mundelein was spared one of those bloody incidents. Instead, he had the troublesome classes of '96 and '97. This collective inkblot wasn't part of any national social or antisocial movement like the longhairs and slackers of the previous eras. They were an independent group of renegade hell-raisers. A class or two of such unpredictable, free-forming human tornadoes can be the most troublesome of all from an administrative perspective because they lacked a purpose or goal. There were no symbolic carrots such as tolerating bell-bottoms to calm them the heck down, nor was there a need to inspire them out of their somnolent doldrums. They were "inspired" enough at it was. Trying to pinpoint a solution was not the kind of headache a principal needs as he's preparing to put the period at the end of a solid and rewarding career.

"We had some embarrassing moments," Davis understates.

As was his style, Davis was hoping the students would start blushing at their behavior on their own. "I believe in allowing kids to make decisions about their lives. The teachers and advisors are there to guide, but you have to let the students make the decisions and make their mistakes."

A noble concept, but it's a lot to ask of model citizen teenagers, much less the more rebellious types. Risky as it seemed, Davis insists such a laid-back strategy had worked well for him in the past. Times change, issues are solved, and each new class comes equipped with their own views, wants, demands, and needs. The lack of continuity from one year to the next—sweeping out the old, ushering in the new—can often be the most effective anthropological cure for a high school's ailments.

Yet, even in such a changing, self-correcting environment, there are behaviors that go against the grain. Instead of phasing out, some spread like seeds for bigger nightmares to come. Davis was keenly aware that the storm brewing at Mundelein High in 1996-97 was of this more insidious breed, a tempest that was specifically designed to have a long-term effect. The precedents that the Mundelein classes of '96 and '97 were setting in the way they were tearing apart long-held school traditions looked to be the start of an ongoing erosion.

The grizzled principal has seen so many faces in and around his school over the years that it's hard for him to pinpoint which of those two classes specifically committed what onerous deed. He does recall that they were particularly zealous in their unofficial competition to see who could set the standard for future mischief.

"We have a lot of student traditions at our school designed as ways of displaying school pride, supporting our athletic teams, and showing a sense of family. This includes putting up posters, hanging crepe paper, having pep rallies, hosting sleepovers, and decorating the school to welcome the new classes at the beginning of the year. Often the students try to outdo what the previous class did. This competitive aspect became a particular problem those years as the students began to add negative features. One of those classes splattered dog food everywhere, along with catsup and mustard. There was also garbage scattered about, and some old furniture was put on the roof. The students got into some heated verbal confrontations with the custodial staff that was trying to stop them. The traditional events had suddenly changed from showing school pride, to something that was demeaning, degrading, and embarrassing."

The principal's memory of the chocolate pudding homecoming crowning was that the bucket of goo was dumped over the queen's head. Others don't remember it going that far, but it's easy to understand how the event began to take on a proverbial life of its own. When the newspaper pictures hit, the phone calls rained in from people who had not attended the actual event. Going by the pictures alone, it certainly looked like a dumping.

"A lot of people were unhappy about it," Davis understates again. "It stirred up talk of things going too far. I preferred the old way of having different colored balloons, flowers, or pulling a name out of a box. Still, it wasn't really that bad. It was embarrassing, and the school was teetering because of the one-upmanship aspect, but the kids, in general, were actually better than in the past. The late 1960s/early 1970s were the worst. Much worse. I wasn't seeing a lot of the bad discipline problems like I'd seen back then, and we weren't having the newer problems some other schools were experiencing, like guns and shootings. It was just a lot of foolishness."

Nevertheless, the foolishness was taking a toll. Davis was forced to cancel some long-held events like the Senior Girls Sleepover, and heavily restrict others in order to try to stem the tide. However, he never viewed such harsh remedies as an effective long-term solution. On the other hand, he fully understood that when a tradition goes sour and transforms into something else, it can be a bear to turn around. In sum, he found himself in a real quandary.

Then, seemingly at the darkest, most chocolately moment, a solution rose Phoenix-like from the most unlikely source.

"Fortunately, we had a group of kids who started talking about the poor choices that had been made over the past couple of years, culminating with homecoming. They stepped forward and began to ask questions like 'What can we do to make this a better place?'"

It was the exact kind of response Davis had been hoping for—a self-disgust emanating from the students themselves. Excited as he was about the prospect of change, the veteran educator felt it best to sit back and let the student-led movement continue to develop on its own. If the administration jumped in at that fragile moment, it might turn off the students. He managed to successfully keep his distance to such an extent that he never knew the identities of the Gang of Nine who kicked it off outside Ms. Royer's French class. What he did know was that it was in good hands.

"Our French teacher, Karen Royer, was the type of person students bonded with. Because she was teaching a language class, many of the students took her at various levels through the years, some for all four years. That gave her a familiarity with the student body that most of the faculty lacked. She took notice of the discontent they were feeling, and saw the opportunity to do something about it. Since she was so well-respected and liked, it was a perfect marriage."

Davis said he was aware that Royer had been scrapping full 90-minute French classes to give the return-to-character movement a birthing point. Many other administrators might have frowned upon, and outright stopped, such curricular heresy, but he had the insight to realize she was on to something bigger than French 301. He was similarly pleased when Royer and the students brought football coach John Ahlgrim into the web.

"The goal in those formative times was to basically identify the problem," Davis recalls. "From what I was hearing, the kids viewed it as overall disrespect, embarrassment, and a lack of class among the student body. They wanted to form a better image of the school and its students. Make it a better place, a community, a fun atmosphere that was safe and pleasant. They wanted to bring back the concepts of respect and dignity, and show that they valued the help and support of their teachers.

"At that point, I was invited into the classrooms to listen to them. I found them to be sincere in their goals. They wanted to do something about the problems they were causing. They were willing to invest the time and energy to make the changes. It was all extremely encouraging. The student leaders then asked to hold forums where everyone in the school community could address what they liked and didn't like, and what changes needed to be made. I allowed them to do this because I thought it was obviously the next step in the process."

Like Royer and Ahlgrim, Davis was overwhelmed by the reaction in the forums. "Usually in these cases, you have 5 percent of the students who care a lot about the school, 80 percent who care a little, and 15 percent who could give a rip." The forums proved that with the right momentum, those numbers can be dramatically altered. This was critical because Davis realized that if this was going to take hold, they were somehow going to have to involve all of the students, especially that last problematic 15 percent—the ones doing 99 percent of the vandalism. Without the "burn-outs" buying into the program, it would be doomed from the onset.

"From there, they engaged in a lot of brainstorming and laundry lists. They needed to develop a clear agenda about how to implement this."

However, before any energy could be spent on the hard part—the implementation plan—there were still more political hurdles to jump. And some pretty substantial ones at that. Illinois schools, especially those in the rural areas and deep suburbs, are set up in small districts that often consist of a single institution. Although Davis had considerable authority and leeway, he wasn't the top dog on campus as a principal normally is. Mundelein was a single school district that had its own, on-site superintendent whose sole responsibility was that one high school. Anything remotely controversial would have to go through him. He, in turn, would have to bring it to the school board.

While having an on-site Super peering over one's shoulder can certainly be a thorn in the side of most principals, in this instance, the odd set up actually worked to the students' advantage. Instead of having to appeal to a distant, ivory-tower figurehead with so much on his plate that "no" becomes the easiest and most personally advantageous way to deal with innovative suggestions, Mundelein's superintendent was instead one of the family. Which meant that Mundelein's patriarch was well aware of what was going on. Like Davis, he patiently sat back, watched with interest, and allowed the effort to grow naturally from the ground up. When and if the time came that the groundswell grew strong enough to blow through his door, instead of being a roadblock, he had some huge aces up his sleeve that would actually give the movement the turbo boost it needed to grow into something extraordinary.

Mundelein Superintendent Art "Tee" Newbrough was born in the coal-mining town of Connellsville, Pennsylvania. He wasn't there long enough, however, to take a cue from country western legend Loretta Lynn and proclaim himself a Coal Miner's Son.

"My parents were just passing through. My father never worked in the mines. He was an industrial engineer. We quickly moved to Michigan, St. Louis, Chicago, and Lake County, Illinois." The final stop led to a glorious—and inglorious—athletic career at Deerfield

High where he set the state record for the 440 dash in track, while at the same time laboring on a basketball team that lost a whopping 63 straight games. The latter mark, which will probably last into the next millennium, was due in large part to the fact that Newbrough was in the first class at Deerfield that went through all four years, entering as a freshman the year the school opened in 1960. Being on a start-up team in the basketball hotbed of Illinois helped keep Deerfield in the loser's column until Newbrough's senior year.

Newbrough's next stop was Illinois State University where, like so many budding Midwestern public school administrators, he played football, doubling as a receiver and defensive back. After graduating with a B.S. in education and a master's in guidance and counseling, he eventually returned home to Deerfield High where he became a teacher, counselor, and football coach from 1970 to 1982. He continued his studies, earning a doctorate degree (Ed.D.) in Educational Administration from Northern Illinois University, which helped put him on the administration fast track. He pulled a stint as the assistant to the superintendent and a career consultant at nearby Highland Park from 1984 to 1986, hopscotched to the Principal's position at Carl Sandburg from 1986 to 1995, then circled back to take the superintendent's post at Mundelein in 1996.

That last promotion, while a solid professional achievement, forced him to confront a personal pet peeve. "I really don't like toilet paper as a decorating device," he says with a laugh. "But that has been an opening day tradition at Mundelein, and the community is tolerant of it. We're still working on that."

Newbrough's office is located in the middle of the spacious, twice-expanded, multibuilding, collegelike 37-acre Mundelein campus, placing him a half a school away from the hustle and bustle of the administration wing where John Davis spends his days. The separation, geographically or symbolically, was not enough to distance the superintendent from what was happening at the school when he arrived in the middle 1990s.

"The students in the back-to-back classes of 1996 and '97 were a more difficult clan than others," he concedes. "They were challenging the traditions, stretching the rules, and crossing the lines. There was a core of student leaders that stepped up their misbehaving. It became competitive. They were each asserting their signature on their year. There's no explanation for it. It was just something in the water.

"I suppose I was upset about the pudding crowning," he says with a sigh. "The kids were just having fun, but it made the front page of the newspaper, and some members of the young lady's family remain embarrassed about it. Fortunately, the next class wasn't interested in having those kinds of things going on anymore. They weren't motivated to try and top that. The discussions started outside Karen Royer's French class. That's all true. She shared in the conversations, and with great energy, helped direct them where to go with their ideas so their determination wouldn't get lost or sidetracked."

Newbrough points out that prior to that fateful day in French 301, Mundelein had already started a "Diversity Club" in which concerned students, teachers, parents, and administrators met periodically after school to discuss ways to bring the racially and culturally divided campus back together. "What that organization did in the earlier years was work on ways to give all the different groups, lifestyles, special need students, genders, ages, sexual preferences, cultures, and religions a sense of unity and belonging. They were trying to build a bridge using the concept of community respect, which was similar to what Karen's students were talking about. We made an effort to bring these two organizations together, and get the student government involved as well."

It was clear, however, that it was Royer's unique, grassroots Gang of Nine that was going to seize the torch and run with it.

"I thought it was great," Newbrough said. "It was the perfect nucleus to move toward constructive solutions. After our recent history of negative student leaders, we had a cultural groundswell of students saying 'Hey, we want to be better! We want to feel better.' The kids were reflecting on their environment and generating a positive voice. Karen, in turn, was a wonderful facilitator, a bright, respected teacher astute enough to get behind what she saw developing. Our principal picked up on it and, without interfering, made sure Karen wasn't by herself. He gave her all the support she needed to enable it to grow.

"I was especially elated because I feel you can't initiate these programs from the top down. You have to be aware of the circumstances, encourage positive student leadership, then water the garden. An administrator would have to be crazy to step in and try and stop it."

Which is not to say it would be easy, especially when it became apparent that Royer's students wanted to turn their fast and furious brainstorming into something real—an actual school-sanctioned curriculum with behavior as the subject, taught by the teenagers themselves in a classroom setting.

"It made great sense, but it was controversial," Newbrough acknowledges. "We would have to get the teachers' union leadership behind it, and the school board."

Befitting a unique program, the superintendent had a unique way of dealing with the board, traditionally an often stodgy, politically minded gaggle of overly starched academic lords. "We didn't ask their permission. We just told them about it. We kept them advised as to what we were doing."

The Illinois teachers union, not surprisingly, proved to be far more meddlesome. "John Davis and I worked with them. We had a lot of discussions. They are concerned anytime you tinker with the school day. They viewed it as giving the teachers another assignment. We resolved it by saying we would have a teacher there in the class, but they would not be responsible for the teaching. It would be student led and taught. We also agreed to pay a stipend to the character education teacher leaders who helped develop the curriculum. We wanted to do both those things anyway, so we didn't have to sell our souls to make this work. John Davis did an especially great job working with the union to make this happen."

Once the union was satisfied, it was back to the school board. A report was presented that included the proposed character education classes "packaged into the regular school schedule." The board raised no objections. "They thought it was great," Newbrough recalls.

With everything set, it was time to play the final ace up Newbrough's crowded sleeve. Nearly a decade before, something very interesting had taken place at his old alma mater. In the late 1980s, Deerfield High began experiencing the same upswing in rowdiness that would later stagger Mundelein. In Deerfield's case, an innovative principal came to the same conclusion as the Mundelein juniors. He created and developed his own character education program, a landmark idea that produced stunning results. Buoyed by the dramatic changes at Deerfield, Newbrough borrowed the concept when he snagged the principal's position at Carl Sandburg. There, the program also met with remarkable success in altering antisocial student behavior. In both those cases, the effort worked despite being initiated from the top down. As with typical educational initiatives, it was administratively conceived and designed, then had to be fed like a spoonful of castor oil down the skeptical gullets of the students. Everyone, students and faculty alike, doubted that a similar approach would work at Mundelein because Mundelien's traditions were being dramatically altered, and the "can you top this" sentiment was so strong. While the character education concept was popping up here and there nationally, Mundelein stood alone in attempting to develop it from the bottom up.

At Mundelein, character education was mutating like those popular children's Pokeman characters. Yet, like those temperamental Japanese cartoon 'pocket monsters,' in order to get a handle on the traits, characteristics, and potential of this bold new mutation, there was a vital need to understand what it had been before. Newbrough decided it was time for Karen Royer, John Ahlgrim, John Davis, and the Gang of Nine to take a hard look at what had happened at his alma mater.

CHAPTER 4

A FIRST CLASS MOVEMENT
AT DEERFIELD HIGH

Deerfield High stands a mere 15 miles from Mundelein. So close, yet in the myopic, sheltered world of high school students, so far. While many of the teachers and administrators shared common bonds and bounced professionally between the institutions, for the students, the schools could have been 15,000 miles apart for all they knew or cared. How could a teenager be expected to give so much as a fleeting thought about the goings-on at another campus when there was already a dizzying array of divisions, factions, and separations among the classes and cliques rambling around their own hallways.

Involved as Mundelein's Gang of Nine was, the traditional teen isolation left the character education fact-finding field trips to French teacher Karen Royer, Dean of Students John Ahlgrim, Principal John Davis, and Superintendent Tee Newbrough. What they found at the neighbor school was the exact blueprint they were looking for.

At the end of the 1980s, Deerfield High appeared to be, on the surface, an idyllic environment for any aspiring principal to walk into. Set in an affluent, professional area on the North Shore of Chicago, it was known for high academic and athletic achievement, along with bustling extracurricular activities. Although religiously divided among Protestants, Catholics, and a large Jewish population, this was never an issue, especially after legal and cultural changes in the 1970s and '80s began to phase out virtually any mention of religion in American public schools. When former University of Wisconsin halfback John Scornavacco was asked to take over as principal, he jumped at the opportunity. Then the assistant principal of nearby Highland Park High School, Scornavacco made the leap, even though he had spent 24 years at Highland Park as a teacher, head football coach, athletic director, and administrator. Plus, Deerfield was his school's most hated rival. Academic career advancement usually runs thicker than school colors—even for an ex-football coach.

"When I arrived in 1987, there was a very capable faculty and a talented student body. What I kept hearing, however, was the same refrain, 'Deerfield is a good high school, but . . . ,'" Scornavacco recalls.

The 'but' varied depending upon the speaker. From the students' standpoint, they complained of overly tight discipline and a place "full of rules." Scornavacco checked out their beefs and found them to have merit.

"The school was too 'custodial.' The adults were controlling the students. The kids were rule driven. The assumption was there had to be a lot of rules and disciplinary action or the students wouldn't behave. In turn, the students felt repressed. They felt that their opinions and thoughts weren't being valued, and they weren't receiving a fair hearing. It was difficult for them, for example, to make class schedule changes or wade through other procedures."

In response, Scornavacco noticed that the students were beginning to rebel. "There was a lot of disrespect for property, each other, and the faculty. Plus, the bad language the students were routinely using was a growing problem. The civility just wasn't there. There were a lot of good things happening at Deerfield, but because of these problems, people didn't feel good about the school. It's a principal's responsibility to create an environment where the students, faculty, and staff can all be successful, and that was the challenge I faced.

"At the end of the first year, I invited the faculty members to a series of gripe sessions. After hearing their concerns, we formed a focus group of 12 teachers. These were mostly veterans who were disenchanted and frustrated. I believe strongly in considering the opinions of the cynics on the faculty because they are often the ones investing the most emotion in the school. They aren't always positive, but they care. To me, anger is better than indifference."

Allowing the faculty to vent their spleens—mostly over the lack of respect they were receiving from the pampered, upperclass Deerfield students—was in and of itself a positive step. Scornavacco had created a safe, professionally secure environment for them to do so, and that helped alleviate much of the frustration. As is usually the evolution of such gripe sessions, once everybody spent their anger and identified the problems, the issues turned toward solutions.

Among the teachers in the focus group were: Bob Gottlieb, a talented special education instructor (Sweat Hogs again) whose students were isolated in a room appropriately known as "The Cage"; Fred Fabry, a motorcycle-riding science teacher, and a bit of a rebel himself with whom the students, not surprisingly, could relate; and assistant football coach and counselor Mike Koehler, an ex-Nebraska fullback and grandson of legendary Native American athlete Jim Thorpe. Together with the others, these three concluded that whatever the solution, the entire faculty would have to buy into it. All desired changes in behavior had to be modeled by every adult at the school. Everyone would treat everyone else with dignity and respect, from the administration respecting the faculty, the faculty respecting the students, and the students respecting the custodial staff. They were asking the students to uphold the same standards they were applying to themselves.

"Kids will respond and meet expectations if they are explained and stated in a pro-social approach," Scornavacco insists.

After a series of meetings, the faculty focus group came up with "The Four We's":

1. We treat each other with dignity and respect.
2. We know our audience when communicating and always use appropriate language.
3. We keep our school neat and clean.
4. We solve our problems creatively by stopping, thinking, and discussing our actions.

"Some of those concepts were broad and difficult to measure, while others were measurable, like cleaning the school, and limiting the swearing," Scornavacco noted, stressing that the program was designed to produce both short- and long-term results.

To get there, the teachers decided, with the principal's approval, that they would try to be more tolerant of some aspects of student behavior. For example, instead of telling kids they shouldn't and couldn't cuss, they would instead enlighten them about social settings where different language is expected.

"If then President George Bush (Sr.) was addressing the nation during a press conference, he wouldn't use a profanity," Scornavacco explains. "However, if later that afternoon, he was playing golf and hit his ball into a sand trap, then couldn't get it out after three tries, *then* it might be okay to use a profanity to express his frustration. He's not on camera and not speaking in public, so he knows he can do it there. To apply that, we told the students that the halls and classrooms were public settings like the president's press conference, and they were to use appropriate language there. In the locker room, it was a different atmosphere and the standards would be lower. The important thing for the students is that the teachers would judge it accordingly. The punishment for profanity in the halls or classrooms would be different than what would be handed out, if any, for something said in the locker room. This is the kind of instruction that works with students, a pro-social skill. This, in a nutshell, was how we approached the rebuilding of the student behavior at Deerfield. We didn't want more rules. We wanted to present this to the kids and find out if they felt it was fair. Their response was very positive."

From there, Scornavacco and his teachers had to construct a format and a lesson plan. During a three-day summer workshop, they built a curriculum to present to the students based upon rationale and research. To implement it, they decided to hold periodic 20-minute classes broken down into small groups of 15 to 20 students. It was a unique and highly controversial attempt at making character building an official part of the high school experience. "A day or so before the 1988-89 year started, Bob Gottlieb and some of the others were outside my office. I heard him say, 'Well, what do we call ourselves?' They were throwing out tag names like 'Class Act,' 'Scout Pride' (after the Deerfield Indian Warrior mascot), 'High Five Program,' 'All-Stars,' but nothing grabbed them. I poked my head out and blurted, 'First Class!' I don't know where it came from. I just let it fly. They went with it, and it stuck.

"At that point, even the most frustrated and cynical teachers were getting behind it. The atmosphere was very positive. We decided to hold the kick-off First Class class during second period the opening day of school. The initial lesson was, 'Let's talk about us, our school.' Each teacher was instructed not to read the lesson plan to the students word for word, but to interpret and paraphrase. They were to think about it and bring it to the students."

Just in case some teachers weren't quite with the program, Scornavacco threw in a clever wrinkle. The teachers were ordered to revisit the First Class issue for a few minutes near the end of the seventh-period class. If a teacher had decided to bag the "silly idea" that morning, the students would be scratching their heads and saying "what First Class issue?" during the afternoon session. The students would feel left out, and it would get back to Scornavacco and the more involved teachers that some of their peers weren't participating. "The pressure would be placed upon the teachers by their own kind," Scornavacco says with a laugh. "Retraining the teacher's thinking was one of the most difficult parts. For example, we discussed this scenario: What if a student came to class with a T-shirt that said 'F-You!' What should a teacher do? The normal reaction of a teacher would be to take immediate disciplinary action because they saw it as a personal insult to them, a 'What could he have been thinking when he put on that shirt? Didn't he realize I would never accept that?' I would explain that when a student gets dressed in the morning, he's not thinking about that particular teacher. The new reaction would be for the teacher to take the student aside and say, 'That shirt is offensive to some people. You are not showing them dignity and respect by wearing it. What do you think you should do about it?' The student would then say, 'Uh, I have a jacket in my locker. I can wear that.' And the teacher would then excuse him to go get his jacket instead of sending him to the dean. If the student takes off the jacket before his next class, that teacher would treat it the same way. Pretty soon he's going to keep the jacket on just to stop being hassled about it. Of course, if the student gets aggressive and refuses to cover it when given the chance, then he goes to the dean. But we first gave him a chance to solve the problem himself, and we didn't get in his face in an adversarial manner to start off.

"These are not real pearls of wisdom, nothing new, but it being a school setting, such faculty behavior can indeed be novel."

The Deerfield principal recalls the student reaction to the First Class program as being positive from the start. "The kids were like, 'What's going on? What's this all about?' The whole school was talking about being 'First Class.' They quickly realized that instead of a crackdown, it was going to mean less rules. It was flipping a pancake. No one expected an immediate turnaround, but we could see from the start we would get there faster than anticipated. There were many almost instantaneous changes. Teachers and students began to treat each other equally with respect. There was a marked reduction in profanity. The halls and the cafeteria were cleaned up almost overnight. If a teacher asked a student to pick up some trash, there was no back talk. The peer pressure for a student to be confrontational was not there anymore. It was almost too good to be true.

"It worked so fast because we gave students a sense of responsibility for their behavior. It was a proactive movement, not reactive."

After that first year, Scornavacco reports that the First Class program was indeed producing measurable results. There was a 56 percent decease in behavior-related referrals to the dean; 54 percent decrease in referrals based upon profanity; 36 percent decrease in referrals related to insubordination; a whopping 100 percent decrease in aggressive language used against a teacher or administrator; and a 37 percent decrease in overall suspensions.

"You simply don't get those results with a custodial, adversarial administrative environment. You get them with the humanistic program we had developed," Scornavacco says.

As with Mundelein, Scornavacco points out that the toughest job was changing long-held student traditions. "We have one at our school where the seniors wear wild T-shirts on their last day of school. Most of them were wildly suggestive, covering sex, drinking, you name it. There was that popular 'Johnson' series (along with the ducks' 'Flying United', the pigs' 'Making bacon,' etc.), those kinds of things. It would be a hassle all day long as some teachers tolerated it, while others didn't. The students would argue and talk back. Well, this flew in the face of the First Class program, so we had to do something about it. We decided to meet them at the door. If the shirt was too over-the-top, we took their name and collected it from them, then gave it back at the end of the day. There was not one single argument that I recall. Because of the First Class program, the students knew it was the right thing to do. They were able to keep their tradition without pushing it too far."

Again, like Mundelein, homecoming was another hot button. "After years of trouble, we instituted a policy that my old school, Highland Park, and Deerfield couldn't schedule each other for homecoming because of the intense rivalry. We had the typical problem of the students visiting each other's schools and trashing the place or destroying each other's parade floats. We also had problems before and after the football games, fights and posturing, things like that. In 1989, the students came to us and asked that they be allowed to have homecoming against Highland Park again. They said they would be 'First Class' about it. I told them they could try it, but only on a test basis that one year. The students agreed. A few of the student leaders got on the school's closed-circuit television and explained that there would be no more late-night visits to Highland Park to vandalize, no more float destroying, and no more bad behavior at the game. Even if Highland Park did it to us, we would not reciprocate. 'This is Deerfield and we are 'First Class,' they announced. Everything went fine, just as they promised, and we've allowed them to renew the tradition of having homecoming against Highland Park ever since.

"My favorite story happened in 1996," Scornavacco recalls. "Our basketball team went 27-1 that year, led by a star player named Ryan Hogan who later played at Iowa and Kentucky. We made it to the 'Sweet 16' of the state finals being played at Northwestern University. We were pitted against this school that was notorious for their outrageous fan behavior. They would do negative cheers, and jeers, and find out specific things about opposing players and taunt them for it. Say a player had an unusual physical feature like big ears, a large nose, bad skin, etc., or was unattractive. They'd ride him unmercifully. Even their cheerleaders would do taunts. It was like what the Duke University students are noted for. Usually, the other school fires back. We decided to go there and cheer with 'First Class' for our team. No matter how much we were taunted and baited, we wouldn't respond. That's exactly what happened. We lost the game, but came away with so much more. The next day, Ryan went on the school's television and said, 'Last night, Deerfield didn't lose. Your behavior made us out to be winners. Today, to celebrate our victory there will be free pizza in the cafeteria!' You could hear the students cheering throughout the building. It was a wonderful moment! It proved to me, more than anything, how deeply the First Class program was taking effect. The students valued their behavior more than winning an important basketball game.

"By the third year, the football team asked to wear the First Class logo we developed on their helmets. It was the word 'First' with a number one over it and the word 'Class.' A student designed it. I was proud that the football team put it on their helmets. That said a lot.

"Another time, a football player came to me and said his younger brother played on an area junior high basketball team. During one of their games, he noticed that a Deerfield teacher's son was playing for the other team. He said the female teacher was yelling and screaming at the officials and acting very un-First Class, and it bothered him. I asked him 'Do you want to talk to the teacher or me?' He said, 'I don't know. I should, I guess.' I asked him if he could address the teacher with respect and dignity. 'I think I can.' He did, and it turned out to be a very uplifting experience. Because he mentioned the First Class program, she was disarmed and wasn't defensive. 'I can't argue with you,' she told him. 'I do get caught up in those games. You're right. I'll try to be better.' He felt very good about it. He liked the fact that he had options, and chose to face it on his own. She told him she appreciated him bringing it up.

"Similarly, I had some junior girls tell me another story. They were at a softball game watching their boyfriends play. They were sitting near the girlfriends of the other team's players. They came back and told me, 'You know, we were never aware how much profanity and how abusive we can be to each other. Those other girls were horrible. You know what? That's not cool.' I was so proud of them!"

Scornavacco's experience with the softball girls is reminiscent of what military recruits often go through in today's society. Thomas Ricks wrote a memorable article in the *Wall Street Journal* in 1995 that touched upon this. Interviewing Marine recruits who had endured 11 weeks of boot camp at Parris Island, Ricks found that their perspective had changed remarkably. (Former U.S. Secretary of Education William Bennett quoted Rick's article in a speech on honor that he presented to the United States Naval Academy in 1997.) "It was horrible," Ricks quoted a graduate referring to his illuminating trip home after camp. "The train was filled with smoke, people were drinking and their kids were running around aimlessly." A second private added, "It was crowded. Trash everywhere. People were drinking, getting into fights. No politeness whatsoever. I didn't let it get to me. I just said, 'this is the way civilian life is.'" A Sgt. Major at the base Ricks spoke to was well acquainted with that disquieting experience among his men. "It is a fact of life that there isn't a lot of teaching in society about the importance of honor, courage, and commitment. It's difficult to go back into a society of 'what's in it for me?'"

Difficult for Marines—and for Deerfield High graduates of the 1990s.

"Of course, we couldn't win over every student," Scornavacco cautions. "You never can. But the program affected even those who didn't realize it. Some kids were outside the bookstore one afternoon and one of them shot a wad of trash into the trash can basketball style. He missed. Another student said jokingly, 'Hey, that's not First Class.' They all had a big laugh. Meanwhile, the shooter went over and picked it up and put it in the can. When a student told me that story, I responded that it was great. They could laugh all they wanted as long as they picked up the trash. If it had been the previous year, they would have left it there on the ground."

As principals go, Scornavacco's insight into the program he created and named is more student-oriented than that of most desk-bound administrators. Still, Mundelein's Karen Royer and gang needed an even more hands-on perspective from someone in the academic trenches. They focused on Koehler, the ex-Nebraska fullback who was Deerfield's long-time assistant football coach. As previously mentioned, the outspoken ex-jock was on Deerfield's original planning committee for the First Class program. He had solid ties to Mundelein as well. Both his daughters had been star athletes at Mundelein in the 1980s, no doubt inheriting their ability from the great Olympian Jim Thorpe. (Thorpe's middle daughter was Koehler's mother.) While wearing one hat as a Mundelein parent, Koehler wore many others for 29 years at Deerfield, holding various positions from teacher to counselor to administrator. Thus, his perspective from the First Class foxhole is especially invaluable.

"There were serious problems with student disrespect before Scornavacco arrived," he concedes. "There was a lot of swearing, and the relationship between the students and teachers was mutually disrespectful. We football coach types figured we'd solve the problem by grabbing the students by their ears and saying, 'Hey, knock it off!' But cracking heads and grabbing ears didn't always work. It never worked with me when I was in school. All it does is make kids rebel more. So I was receptive to trying something new, this concept of internal self-discipline over external discipline and punishment. The motivation to behave must be internal. But you can't go to the other extreme—the hands off, laissez-faire way of dealing with kids either.

"I had been right in the heart of it during the 1960s when the times suddenly changed and the issue of student behavior came to a head. There were a lot of angry people back then, both students and teachers. The values of the '40s and '50s were being rejected, and the students and parents were left confused as to what was happening. Kids were tired of being told what to do, how to dress, how to talk. There was a popular essay at the time entitled 'The Student as a Nigger' that really inflamed the passions. It encouraged students to rebel and, by God, they did! Clothing, hair, short skirts, see-through blouses, talking back—they did as they damn well pleased. In turn, the administration tried to crack down. The administrators and teachers would actually make the girls kneel on the floor. If their skirts didn't touch the back of their legs, they would be sent home to change. Not surprisingly, the students protested. We had two sit-down strikes at Deerfield over the dress code alone. They sat down in the halls and wouldn't move. The administrators wanted to call the cops, but I talked them out of it. We eventually ended up meeting with the students, and loosening the dress and hair codes, just like everybody else. We didn't have much choice.

"That created a subsequent 'values vacuum.' The kids had rejected the old ways, morals, and guidelines, but didn't know how to replace them. Parents and teachers surrendered. Laissez-faire kicked in, leading to an age of permissiveness. There were some tough times. Fortunately, the football arena stayed pretty much the same. Football is a sport based upon discipline. The players needed discipline to satisfy their own egos and need for accomplishment, so they were immune to what was happening everywhere else. And what was happening everywhere else was a startling contrast."

It was this multifaceted perspective that prompted Koehler, who holds a Ph.D. in Educational Administration, to volunteer to be a member of Deerfield's original character education focus group. "We wanted to teach kids to understand and be able to say to themselves,

'I know the right thing to do and I have the character to do it. I can be a first-class person. We can make the school a first-class organization. We can respect each other.' You've got to give John Scornavacco his due, because it caught on. We suddenly had a clean school. The kids were putting trash in the garbage. That never happened before. I remember after the first year, I was walking down the halls and noticed something unusual. I went to Scornavacco's office and said, 'The homecoming decorations are intact. I guess this First Class program is a good idea.' We all started feeling the same way. The students embraced it because they were part of it. We had students on the steering committees. We were engaging the kids.

"As routine as this sounds, there are an awful lot of schools in this country that are not thinking in these terms. It's that laissez-faire thing again. Education in this country is a mess. We are only one small area of Illinois that did something about it. The contrast is the permissive approach that leads to what happened at Columbine where kids are making pipe bombs in the basement and their parents don't know about it. That's why parents love the First Class program. A majority of parents are lost and confused about child rearing. They want to be pals, not parents. So they loved what we were doing.

"Tee Newbrough was aware of our program a few years after it started, and he brought it to Carl Sandburg High School in Orland Park when he became principal there. That's why I wasn't surprised when I heard that they were going to institute it at Mundelein. I know it was a student-driven movement there, which makes it a special case, but you can't overlook the fact that everywhere Tee was, the First Class program soon followed."

Knowing that, Mundelein Principal John Davis dispatched a committee to check out what was happening at Carl Sandburg, and brought some of the Sandburg students and teachers over to his school as well.

"That gave us more impetus and momentum in what we wanted to do," Davis said. "We decided to develop a First Class program. We didn't see a reason to be unique or different, or even to change the name. Plus, Tee knew that system. He was involved the whole way. Our school board was very supportive and hands off. They were briefed on what we were doing through 'information items' or 'action items' and proposals, and always gave their support. They eventually approved stipends for the teachers on the planning committee."

Football coach John Ahlgrim was among those who made the trek to the rival institutions. "I was very impressed with how First Class had become part of the infrastructure of their school day. We also thought, 'Boy, there are things we want to change when we bring it back to Mundelein.' The time frame was one. They were having it every week, and we were kind of hesitant about that. We thought that might be too much. Another aspect involved the grade levels. Carl Sandburg had their character education classes segregated by the grades. We decided not to go that way. We wanted to mix our kids in order to break down the divisions we were experiencing. At our assemblies, one class was yelling about another class, and we wanted to put an end to this verbal sign of differences. Our students were taking pride in their differences rather than their similarities, which was counterproductive."

To gain insight on how a First Class program progresses through the years, the Mundelein task force returned to Deerfield and huddled with Scott Kasik, the teacher/administrator Scornavacco chose to oversee its long-term development.

"I've been actively involved with First Class for eight years," the Western Illinois graduate says. "I was supportive from the beginning. There was some teacher opposition in the early days, the 'that's not my job' belief that student behavior, especially regarding how they treat each other, was out of the realm of a teacher's responsibility. Some felt they didn't have the time, or weren't happy with the added work. Faculty groups as a whole tend to be suspicious of any new program. They question whether it will have longevity. It was important that this was presented to them in a manner where they knew it would not be a flash-in-the-pan. We encouraged them to talk it over among themselves, and gave them the time to attend workshops.

"Teachers are usually comfortable controlling their classrooms, but don't feel the same way when dealing with students they don't know in the hallways or cafeteria. The old reaction was, if they heard bad language in the halls, they'd shut their doors. Now we wanted them to address it, and we needed to set up a program that enabled them to address it in a nonconfrontational matter. Our plan raised eyebrows because it's often difficult to get the staff to accept something that gives students more control. On top of that, we adults would be expected to set an example by being calm and respectful as well. We couldn't just give lip service to the First Class ideals. And it would be easy to treat the good kids, the model citizens, with respect. The hard part was treating the bad kids that way. We had to include everybody in the program, even the kids on the fringes. If we respected them all, the kids would all respond. And they did."

Kasik, who took over as Deerfield's principal when Scornavacco retired prior to the 2000-2001 school year, plans to continue what his innovative predecessor started.

"First Class is an easy program for kids to accept because they feel more empowered. They have the incentive of improving the climate and color of their environment, and it's not designed to be something forced down their throats. When we started having discipline problems, we could have cracked down tighter. That's the easy fix. Just add more discipline. But we didn't want to do that. We wanted the kids to take responsibility for themselves. For example, instead of just putting them in detention for using bad language, we explained to them why it was better not to use those words. We reminded them that there were others in hearing range like parents, college representatives, and small children from the employee day care center. We asked them to please monitor their language accordingly. That feels better to them than punishment. We gave them a way they could buy into it."

The structure, frequency, and timing of First Class changed over the years at Deerfield as administrators refined the concept. "We never wanted kids to think it was just one 20-minute class once a week," Kasik explains. "First Class is all day all the time. It's integrated into the total curriculum. It's taught by the coaches as part of football, basketball, and the other sports as well. It encompasses a student's entire daily life. We have something called Freshman Advisory that's a required class for our freshmen. It is not a direct part of the First Class program, but is designed to be a similar home base. It's a nonacademic homeroom setting that acts as a safe haven. They meet every day to discuss drugs, alcohol, AIDS, dating, adjusting to high school, study skills, peer pressure, etc. We do use the Freshman Advisory as a vehicle for informing students about the school culture, but our First Class discussions are only a part of the advisory curriculum."

Both First Class and its close cousin, Freshman Advisory, feed upon reverse reinforcement.

"We as teachers wanted to catch kids being good as opposed to being bad," Kasik points out. "As a reward, we did things for them.

Sometimes we'd give out free popcorn to thank them for 'being First Class.' You can smell it cooking all over the school, so that's really effective. Fifty dollars can buy a ton of popcorn. We also had a coupon program where we gave students coupons redeemable in the bookstore for pens, First Class logos, candy bars, whatever they wanted. They love getting things for free. They may be in high school, but they're still kids.

"To keep the enthusiasm high and momentum going, we have special events and anniversary parties. We play a version of 'Who Wants to Be a Millionaire' only it's 'Who Wants to Be First Class?' We play other silly and fun games like having races on these little bikes. Once a month, we have the teachers bring cookies and other treats and sit with the students in the cafeteria during lunch. We gave all the teachers and staff a nice red Polo shirt with the First Class logo on it. That included the custodial staff because it's important to always include them. The adults wear them periodically during the year, and many have taken to wearing them every Friday. We also gathered the teachers, administrators, and staff and took a photograph of everybody in their shirts. The shirts went over so big that the students were clamoring for their own. We ended up designing something a little different for them. The shirts, events, celebrations are all about building a community.

"On the other hand, you don't want to beat it to death. We've also learned when to pull back. Nobody can be 'up' all the time. We never want to reach the point where the students say 'enough already!' So there's a delicate balance."

"Beating it to death" was not a problem the Mundelein crew would have to face for a few years. They were more worried about tugging the cord hard enough to crank a brand new engine from a dead start. To that end, they were now armed with the extensive experience gained at Deerfield and Carl Sandburg, and were buoyed by the fact that their superintendent was on board even more enthusiastically than he originally let on. Karen Royer, John Ahlgrim, and the rest of the Mundelein task force returned home ready to bring First Class to their hungering student body.

CHAPTER 5

DEVELOPMENT AND LIFTOFF

With a successful model to build upon, Mundelein teacher Karen Royer and football coach John Ahlgrim plunged ahead. Their first challenge was to regain the momentum lost during the summer of '97. In the world of fickle teens, last week's hot topic can be this week's old school joke, and it was now three long, fun-filled months later. Would the juniors have the same enthusiasm to right the ship that they had in May? Did the heat of summer combine with the idle, aimless days to cool their passion for goodness and light and usher in a sense of indifference? And scarier yet, did their more wild and radical classmates knock some sense into their cloud-nine heads and convince them that this whole concept of being squeaky clean and respectful was majorly Geek City? Did the Class of '98 really want to willingly give up their hard-earned gains and loosened restraints and passively turn the school back over to the starched, anal-retentive assistant principals of the world?

This was, after all, their senior year, a once-in-a-lifetime opportunity to reign supreme, bully the weak, and raise copious amounts of youthful hell. It would be their last hurrah as mischievous teens allowed to act up in a protected environment before they faced the cold realities and harsher rules of the big bad world. Did they seriously want to spend this precious time turning into choir boys and girls?

"I didn't know how it would turn out at that point," Ahlgrim admits. "There was a certain degree of skepticism sinking in. There was the feeling that kids inherently don't like to be lectured about their behavior. The positive side to counter that was this time the message was going to be delivered by their peers."

Cleverly, Royer, Ahlgrim and the Gang of Nine knew better than to give into the skepticism of their fellow teachers, and their own self-doubts, and kept pushing the positives. Before the 1996-97 year ended, they had already taken steps to combat a possible summer-blonde countermovement.

"We asked the students and faculty to identify 100-plus juniors they felt would be good leaders," Royer explains. "These were students with strong values who we believed could interact with their classmates in a good way. They would be the ones to kick off the First Class program at Mundelein."

Ahlgrim especially enjoyed this process. "The reason I like coaching football is that I have input in developing players as leaders. If they are enthused or excited by the role, it becomes a means to explain why it's important to follow the rules. It's not delivered from a perspective of intimidation, but through a message of 'I care about you enough to make the right decisions.' This is the way I felt when we were selecting that initial group of First Class Student Leaders. We were looking for kids with good values, good communication skills, and good judgment. I suggested the students who I knew well, kids like Luke Hajzl and Bill Zasadil, young men who wanted to rise up to another level. The coaches and faculty advisors for student government and the various after-school clubs were similarly important in this process because we were able to see the students interact in different arenas. As with me, they could identify those who had already emerged as leaders."

That, as it turned out, was the easy part. The hard part would be what to do with them after they were selected.

"We set a time during the summer where they would come in for training," Royer said. "As far as I know, every student we selected accepted the challenge."

They accepted in the spring, that is. There remained the question of how many would actually show with pencils in hand during the dog days of summer when the bell rang for the intensive, volunteer summer sessions. That mystery would have to wait. There were more immediate hurdles to jump, like preparing an administration-pleasing curriculum for both the training sessions, and the actual First Class program.

In this area, Royer continued to receive unqualified support from the other end of the Mundelein spectrum. "We had the go ahead from the administration to proceed as fast and far as we could with this. That's a vital component because unless you have support from the entire school community—students, faculty, administration and parents—the chances of success are limited."

What was also needed for success was a concrete way to implement a still hazy concept. Royer and Ahlgrim joined with a smaller group of students and teachers to develop an actual classroom strategy. The teachers who stepped forward were Jose Acosta, Jodi Cusick-Acosta, Susan Theotokatos, Kathy Hajek, Kathy Bell, Linda Paulus, Karen Hall, Karen Chilcote, Dave Ekstrom, Mary Jane Chiado, Judy Juske, Alexander Kapotas, Lillian Medina, Brian Swanson, and Jodi Wirt.

"I signed on because they were paying a stipend, $60 a day I believe, for the four-day summer planning session," Ekstrom confesses. "I supported the concept and all, but the money was a big part of it. I wouldn't have done it if it was strictly volunteer. There was a lot of work involved, and I was already busy coaching both the girls and boys soccer teams."

Ekstrom, a Physical Education and Driver Education teacher, recalls having to create the curriculum from ground zero. "We spent those four days mapping out the whole thing: the name, mission statement, lesson plans for the first semester, class schedule, times, everything. We were inventing it as we went along."

Ahlgrim, Ekstrom's fellow coach, felt the same way. Despite their illuminating trips to Deerfield and Carl Sandburg, Mundelein's bottoms-up version of First Class involved razing the field and building a foundation from brick one. "It was a hard game to play trying to figure out how to get the kids involved in conducting the actual classes. That's why we asked the students. We needed their input into the lesson plans. We didn't want to create more rules. Even as a football coach, where discipline is critical, I wasn't the type to create too many laws because that doesn't always work.

"One of the goals of First Class was to change the students' language. That was something I'd had a lot of experience with because football is an aggressive sport where some might accept bad language as an overall part of this aggression. I've never agreed with that. I've always been committed to the idea that bad language is not appropriate anywhere, in the hallways or on the football field. If a coach allows it to creep in, there's a hidden message that the language is okay. And if one teacher or coach accepts it, it's harder for the another to correct it.

"On the field, if I heard my players speak that way, I could run them, make them stay after practice and do push-ups; punitive measures like that. However, I preferred to just explain to them that 'this is wrong and it will not be tolerated.' They usually responded to that because it gets to the heart of the matter. This was similar to the way we wanted to approach things with First Class."

Developing such philosophical instructional frameworks was vital, but as Ekstrom noted, they were still planning everything from scratch. The basic structure of the program had to be worked out before the initial clean-language discussion could take place. To this end, the first thing the faculty/student committee decided was to follow the Deerfield model and hold class once a week for a conservative 20 minutes—kind of a miniperiod—with the time shaven bit by bit from the rest of the school day. They also reiterated an earlier decision not to separate the students by year as is normally done with homerooms. In all, there would be 94 classes of 16 students each, four from each grade.

"Most of the students' classes were already isolated enough," Royer emphasizes. "The kids didn't get to know each other as individuals. In the First Class program, we wanted them to merge across class-year boundaries. We decided to have 16 students per session, four from each grade level. We wanted them to relate as people, not seniors, juniors, sophomores, and freshmen. The point was to break down group stereotypes and turn it into something more like a family dinner table with the older sisters and brothers bonding with their younger siblings. Maybe, like younger siblings, the freshmen and sophomores would be initially intimidated and stay quiet, but once in a while they might drop gems of wisdom that amazed the rest of the gathering. In addition, like a family, they would form bonds of friendship and trust that penetrated class divisions.

"As for the lesson plans, we started with the basics. We began with the premise that nobody would come in with an inherent knowledge of how to behave in school, how to behave at assembly, how to behave in the cafeteria, and what language was appropriate to use in the hallways. It was amazing the bad language you'd hear the students use. A lot of times, the kids didn't even know that what they were saying was so bad. They'd heard it so often on television or in movies, videos or music. Those words seemed normal to them. Our goal was to establish new behavior by applying the lessons in a variety of ways: role-playing situations, discussions, and allowing them to form their own rules and their own concept of right and wrong. Each lesson would have a clear message and core content, but it would be an ongoing process. We expected to be constantly revising, revisiting, and tweaking it to see what worked.

"What helped is we were left on our own from an administrative standpoint. Tee Newbrough's earlier encouragement was applied here as well. 'Go with it and see what happens. Take it as far as you can go.' We met with John Davis regularly and he let us design and prepare what we thought was appropriate as a committee."

There were, however, unspoken issues that Royer knew she would have to dance around—religion being the most sticky. Mundelein students were a diverse group of Catholics, Protestants, Fundamentalists, Baptists, Muslims, even some Hindus. Despite this, she doesn't recall anyone on the committee trying to push their own set of religious-based morality into the First Class program.

"Religion has been separated from our schools," Royer accurately states while missing the irony that her school, and the city it serves, took its name from a Catholic Cardinal. "Students today have been conditioned not to discuss religion. We've shied away from saying what's right and wrong based upon traditional religious values. We teach that lying and cheating is wrong, not because it goes against a religious belief, but because it's just wrong. And that's whether someone is watching or not. We teach that there needs to be an attitude of tolerance based upon understanding who we are as people. Our skin or religion doesn't make us more or less important than someone else. So this is the way we would deal with the subject if it came up during First Class."

To everyone's relief—except maybe the spirit of Cardinal Mundelein—the concern over pumping the First Class program with sect-based morality never materialized.

"The religious issue simply didn't become an issue, even with the students," notes Royer, a Lutheran Church choir member. "In our situation, racism was a bigger issue and a lot stronger topic. Everyone's religion has the basic tenet of respect for self and others, and that was what we were going to teach. It doesn't matter what religion you are if you have respect for yourself and for others. We were going to teach basic values. Plus, it wasn't the intent of First Class to be in competition with the various after-school clubs where religion is allowed."

Aside from understanding that religion was a topic too hot to handle for public schools, Royer had her own personal experiences with its divisive side. "My husband is Roman Catholic and I was raised Methodist. His parents had a hard time with our relationship. His priest told him straight out to find someone else to marry. For years, my husband would attend two churches on Sunday. He'd go with us to the Methodist Church, then alone to his Catholic Church. One day our children asked me if our church wasn't good enough because Dad was going to a different one. That opened our eyes. After that, we shopped for a faith we could all share. We decided that Lutheran fit, plus they had a strong youth group."

To avoid a similar scenario stirring overheated emotions in her fragile and infant First Class program, Royer developed a game plan that stressed social topics and general character-building exercises, with an emphasis on getting feedback from the students. Since these would be small groups chosen at random from the entire mixture of the student body, each class could have a decidedly different ethnic and religious makeup. Therefore, personal beliefs aside, tackling religion would be difficult to accomplish across the board anyway. First Class instead would be designed around the students' ideas and concerns first and foremost. Besides, teenagers rarely bring up the topics of death or religion themselves.

What turned out to be a bigger problem was making sure all the Mundelein teachers—atheists or devout—were fully on board. A few renegade teachers could have a disproportionately damaging effect.

"We had to take into consideration that, as a rule of thumb, 10 percent of the teachers weren't going to be able to pick up the ball and run with it," Royer acknowledges. "Some felt threatened by the whole concept. It made them uncomfortable to have to deal with anything outside of their specialties, especially character issues. They felt that it wasn't their job to take a stand on right and wrong and morals, only math and science. This faction felt that the kids should learn their character and morals at home. We countered that we, as teachers, are responsible for the whole student, their value system as well as their education.

"We also anticipated that some teachers would find it difficult to sit back and turn their classes over to the students. Others wouldn't be comfortable with the fact that there would be no grade to hold over a student's head. Whatever their reason for being unhappy or uneasy, we figured these teachers wouldn't spend the time that was necessary to work with their designated Student Leader. They would view that as above and beyond what they were hired to do."

With booby traps seemingly everywhere, the planning for that first year was complicated and intense. Royer had to consider all possibilities and scenarios, positive and negative. "To counter these and other problems, we took some of the best student leaders and created the 'M-Team'—the 'M' standing for Mustangs (the school's mascot). They would serve as roamers—strong, outgoing leaders who would 'roam' to classes that were floundering because of a weak student leader, an uncooperative teacher, or listless students. They would be specially trained to be of assistance, but not make the class leader or teacher feel threatened in their position."

It all seemed like a lot to chew on, and the engine promised to be filled with start-up glitches. Nonetheless, Royer and gang powered on, convinced that the bumps could be smoothed over as long as the enthusiasm and desire was kept high. That, as previously mentioned, was the million-dollar question. Would the potential student leaders even show for training?

"Late that summer, we invited the students we'd selected the previous spring, promising pizza and Cokes for lunch. 'Feed them and they will come,' and they did. They all came! We had three daylong, off-campus sessions in leadership training and conflict resolution. Basically, they were taught how to handle people in discussion groups and get them involved. Plus there was extra training for those who would comprise the M-Team. The kids were great. They arrived ready and motivated. They still wanted to make a mark on the school."

If nothing else, the fact that more than 100 incoming seniors were volunteering to give up their last precious days of summer to attend training sessions was itself miraculous.

"I was surprised by the turnout," Ahlgrim confesses. "It had an added effect on me because, as a dean, I was always dealing with misbehavior and discipline problems—the negative end. All day long, that's what I was seeing, and that can give you a tainted view about your school. I was overwhelmed to see, as a contrast, a large gathering of responsible, polite, involved students who knew how to behave, and wanted to learn how to teach their peers to behave. This was a refreshing example of the kind of students that comprised the majority, the good kids I never saw in my office. Watching them that summer inspired me to increase my role in First Class to a greater degree. It put a new light on things. In the midst of a problem, here was the solution."

Principal John Davis, ever the optimist, said he never feared that the summer doldrums would hamstring the momentum from the previous spring.

"I wasn't really that shocked by the attendance. Because of all the buildup, I saw it growing. I could see their commitment at the earlier meetings. Their motivations were altruistic and true. Everyone was jumping on the bandwagon. I was elated. It was exciting to watch it develop. I could see the potential for this kind of thing."

The students saw the potential as well, so much so they were willing to cut their summer short.

"I didn't have a problem with giving up the time," Julie Waskey, '98, confirms. "It was something that was worthwhile and good for the school. The sessions were about how to get us to be leaders. We did skits and ice-breaker exercises aimed at getting us to be more relaxed in front of a class. It was okay. Some of it was a little silly, maybe. I'm not sure we really used anything that we learned in the training, but I'm sure it was helpful in some way."

Original founder Billy Zasadil was playing baseball that summer but tried to squeeze in as much of the training as he could. "I'd drive right from the games to catch the last hour or so. It was in the basement of a bank, or something like that, in a new building. I don't know why it wasn't at school. As I recall, they taught us skills that would help us lead a group, how to come to conclusions within a circle, and how to facilitate discussion and not dominate. What I do remember is there was a huge participation. The room was full of incoming seniors."

Luke Hajzl (Hay-zel), '98, a football fullback/linebacker who was one of Coach Ahlgrim's selections, wedged the training into his busy schedule as well. "We were different than the previous seniors. We were into the school, so we liked the whole concept of the First Class program. We weren't going to be out there beating up the freshmen and dorks. Maybe we wouldn't be hanging out with them, but we weren't going to bang on them either. Giving up a few days of summer was no big deal, and Coach Ahlgrim was part of it. He asked some of us football players to support it out of respect for the teachers.

"We learned some interesting things in the training and small group exercises. What I remember was the aspect of using 'I' to diffuse problems. Instead of being accusatory and saying something like 'You cheated me!' you'd say, 'I feel that you cheated me.' Instead of 'You hurt me,' it would be 'I'm hurt by that.' Instead of saying 'You bastard, you never liked me anyway,' you ask 'What did I do to you to cause these feelings?' I felt those were good concepts."

Thanks to Royer's "good concepts" and astute planning, combined with the students' unwavering enthusiasm, the "founders" had indeed managed to keep the momentum rolling through the summer. But just in case, Royer had one more trick up her French-cut sleeve, something right out of Hollywood.

"The day before school started in August 1997 we held a school-wide teachers meeting in the cafeteria to explain to the faculty what was going to happen starting the next day in regards to the First Class program. We had committee leaders outline what it was, what we wanted to accomplish, the curriculum we developed, and told the short history of how it all began. I could see by their expressions that many of the teachers were skeptical."

At the same time, something very interesting was going on outside. The teachers began to hear a low rumble coming through the walls.

"After we told them about the summer training program, and how overwhelming the response was from the chosen Student Leaders, we walked to the doors and threw them open. 'And now here they are!' At that moment, more than 100 trained and enthusiastic First Class Student Leaders poured through the doors and filled the room. It was so exhilarating, like a scene from a movie! The students filtered in and sought out their assigned First Class teachers, who were sitting there with their initial lesson plan in hand. They immediately formed 100-plus private, two-person teams to discuss how the next day would go.

"It was a huge shot in the arm for everybody. Virtually all the skeptical teachers changed their minds right then and there. Even the most doubtful said, 'Well, maybe this will work.' I heard so many positive comments, 'This is so exciting,' 'This is just what we need,' 'This is great!' The teachers were impressed with the caliber, energy, and determination of the kids."

So far, so good, but unfortunately, a double whammy of acid tests would come before the first First Class student put his fanny in a seat. There remained that little matter of decorating the school later that evening, and the opening day assembly—both sore spots from Mundelein's wild and wooly past.

"It was incredible," Royer recalls. "The school was beautifully decorated with banners and posters welcoming the freshmen. They didn't even toilet paper the trees, which would have been okay. The First Class program hadn't officially started and it already had made a dramatic difference! And the decorations stayed up! No one tore anything down. Then, later at assembly, the classes cheered on cue, and stopped on cue. When they were given the sign to 'cut,' they stopped. That had never happened before in my experience. It was obvious that the seniors were determined to set a precedent right off, and the other classes were following suit. The seniors had revised the whole assembly. And best of all, there were no chants of 'Freshmen Suck.' "

When the 94 individual classes actually started, things went a little less perfectly, to say the least.

"Everybody was tentative as to what to do," founder Jennifer Bouteille recalls, quickly pointing out that she wasn't allowed to be a Student Leader that year because she was an underclassman. "In my group, the leader read the lesson plan right off the page, which was clumsy and stilted. People didn't want to be there. It was hard to get anyone to talk."

Zasadil, who was a leader, said his class struggled as well, only for different reasons. "I had a teacher who was brand new that year, and he kept taking the class away from me. He couldn't let go of his control and wouldn't let me lead as it was designed. There was some bad blood between us because of that. I eventually became a roamer, one of the students who went from class to class. That was better.

"In general, I really liked the way the kids handled themselves, and most of the leaders were talented and personable. They related and connected with their class. Those with the best personalities really shined through and those classes worked great.

"The subjects and topics in the beginning were mostly the concerns we had brought up in Ms. Royer's French class the prior year regarding respect for the school and behaving properly. We received our lesson plans on Monday, which gave us two days to prepare for the First Class on Wednesday. We did some ice-breaker things early on, such as tossing a tennis ball around the group and saying our names and something about ourselves. There was another ice breaker that was kind of corny. We passed around a rolled-up newspaper and tapped each other on the head. When you were tapped, you had to give three "stats" about yourself: shoe size, height, weight, things like that. It didn't go over real well, but we laughed a lot and eventually it succeeded in breaking the ice, which I guess was the whole point. Those games did build a sense of community among us.

"Another good thing was how the classes were divided up to represent all years. I got to know a lot of younger kids I never would have known before. I was the quarterback of the football team, and I wasn't aware of how much the younger kids looked up to me. I wouldn't have experienced it to that degree if it hadn't been for First Class. It made the school seem a whole lot smaller, which was a good thing. Of course, it all seemed to hinge upon the Student Leaders. Some just couldn't lead. Others weren't comfortable being up front. And, as I mentioned, some teachers wouldn't let go. Those classes struggled."

Stumbling blocks aside, what Royer, her fellow teachers, and the Mundelein administration were quickly learning was that even if the individual classes weren't all going perfectly, the effect upon the school as a whole could still be dramatic.

"The homecoming assembly went even better than the opening day assembly," Royer notes. "The students sat with their First Class groups instead of with their classes, so that was a major step in preventing the class rivalries of the past. Most were dressed in the school colors, something we hadn't seen in years. The entire gym was a sea of red and white. The cheers were modified to be positive and supportive of the football team. The students gave the Mustang Battle Cry together instead of competing class against class. They followed the instructions of the cheerleaders. Then, when it came time for each class to have their moment, the other classes stayed quiet and respected them. Again, no 'Freshmen Suck" chants and back and forth insults. At one point, the teachers held up a banner that read 'You Are First Class,' which was met with wild cheers. It was unbelievable!"

Subsequently, the senior girls asked for, and received, the right to have their slumber party again the night before homecoming. "They worked like Trojans the whole evening, decorating the gym and halls without incident," Royer recalls. The next day, the decorations stayed up. Even the ones in the gym remained in place before, during, and after the assembly. Better yet, there were no "Trojans" wrapped around telephones, and no chocolate pudding in sight. Instead, a box was placed at the feet of each of the five homecoming queen finalists. The girls opened the box and the one who found a crown was the queen. "Nice and sweet," notes Royer.

Bouteille, who observed that the individual classes got off to a rocky start, agrees with Royer that the overall effect was positive. "Things were actually better around the school. Homecoming was far more controlled than the previous year. Some people were making fun of the First Class stuff, and the fact that they couldn't shout insults like before, but there was a lot more respect because of it. Students were getting along. And the appearance of the school was totally changed. It wasn't gross with trash all over like before."

"It was a pretty dramatic change," Zasadil concurs. "We had a sense of community, just like we wanted the year before. There was no more tension in the halls and cafeteria because nothing was being held back. Everything was being spit out in First Class. Our super hormone-charged lives were not bottled up like before. We had a place to let it out. You could be pissed off about stuff and not have to stew over it.

"On the other hand, it was still tough to get through to the Mexican kids. That problem was going to take longer to fix. They continued to be standoffish, even in their First Classes. Their culture tells them to keep things to themselves, so it wasn't natural for them to speak up. Plus, some didn't understand English well. But as the year went on, and they got past the 'us against them' thing, they were a lot more involved in the discussions. In turn, they became a lot more involved in the entire school. I started seeing some of these guys at the football games cheering for the team. That was something you never saw before. I think that because of what was going on in First Class, they were starting to feel that they were an important part of the school, part of the whole."

That's an honest assessment, without doubt, from the school's BMOC quarterback, First Class Student Leader, M-Team roamer, and the guy who was at point zero in creating the program to begin with. In a sense, however, Zasadil had become a student version of an administrator. The big question remained: What did the run-of-the-mill students sitting in the First Class chairs really think about the program?

CHAPTER 6

THE STUDENTS REACT

Teenagers, being the contrary creatures they are, usually respond in a highly unpredictable manner to virtually any stimulus. Thus, their opinions on a shared academic experience can conflict to such an extent one might question whether they are referring to the same events. The First Class program falls squarely into this sociological phenomena. The reactions of the pioneers who started the novel movement, along with those of their classmates who went through it, form a rainbow of opinions that cover the entire spectrum.

Shane Chareonchump, '99, the football linebacker and split end whose parents came to Illinois from Thailand, was one of the first underclassmen the original founders recruited. Although he couldn't become a First Class Student Leader until the second year of the program because, at the time, it was limited to seniors, he still had an insider's view of both the development and implementation.

"It was shaky at first. The kids didn't know what to think. We were happy to get out of our other classes a little earlier, but First

Class was kind of childish in the beginning. The ice-breaker games were for kids."

Chareonchump, who went on to Ohio State, agrees with Zasadil that the classes lived and died with the quality of the Student Leader. "The First Class leaders had to take charge. The leader I had that initial year was a really good person, but didn't have the skills for this kind of thing. She wasn't outspoken enough. Plus, our teacher was too involved. He couldn't sit back and let the students run it. He tried to take the lead, and would cut in every few minutes when we got a discussion going. He pushed his thoughts and beliefs as the strongest and most accurate, which was not what the class was supposed to be about. Our peer leader would often sit down and just let him take over. Considering these negatives, the students themselves did actually get pretty involved. I remember we talked about sexual harassment and racism among other things.

"We had some lesson plans that everybody thought were a joke, but they still had an effect. In one, we were told to substitute another word for a swear word. The word they chose was 'marshmallow.' People were yelling 'marshmallow' all over as kind of a joke on the program. You'd even hear it at football practice, 'this marshmallow sucks!' Joke or not, they were saying that instead of something bad, I guess.

"The program did have an effect on the school. Things were sinking in. The level of respect we were showing each other increased, and the atmosphere was better. But that first year there were groups of kids who just rebelled against it. They thought it was stupid and would sit in class and crack jokes and one-liners. Even with that, we still had some good sessions. The second year was a lot better. I was still supportive of it, and I wanted more influence in the school, so I became a Student Leader. Actually, I became an M-Team member, a roamer. I had a conflict with football practice, so I couldn't attend all of the training sessions that summer. Coach Ahlgrim let it slide. I didn't mind giving up some of my summer for this because I was able to see my friends again. They fed us pizza and pop and stuff so it wasn't that bad. I believe it was two days that year. I basically learned a little bit about how to communicate, handle myself, and deal with troublemakers. We learned about putting kids in different groups, moving them around, using seating charts, and playing games that opened people up to talking and sharing. There was a memory game where we tried to remember each other's names and some facts about them—their shoe size, something like that. Another one had us trying to remember things we had in common with each other.

"When these games were applied in the classes, they were effective to the extent that they got everyone involved. They helped break the ice on the first day and allowed everybody to become comfortable with each other.

"What remained important, even the second year, was that everyone had to be aware that this program was generated by the students. We weren't being told to do it. It had been our idea from the start. As the years progressed, it would be critical to keep reminding the new students how it started. The concept of students talking to students has more of an impact. Seeing a student at the front of the class leading the discussions made a huge difference because it was student to student, and that made us respect what was being said and listen more.

"I really enjoyed being a roamer and going to the different classes. I'm not afraid to speak my mind, and people listened. There were four of us roamers that year, and we'd substitute for an absent leader, or reinforce a shy or ineffective one. Sometimes you'd end up with a whole class of shy people, so you had to work to get a discussion going. Other classes were full of rebels or troublemakers. Whatever the problem, we'd usually iron it out and get the class moving. It was nice teaming up with the class leaders because they were usually friends who appreciated the help. I remember one class in particular had a lot of problems with the First Class program itself. They didn't like it. They thought it was childish, moved too slow, and stalled on uninteresting subjects. So I became a mediator between them and their leader and teacher and worked it out so they would get more out of it.

"Overall, I noticed from my freshman year to senior year there was a huge change in the way we behaved. There was no bullying of the freshmen the way I had been pushed around. I attribute that to First Class. And people were always saying 'That's not first class!' about this or that. It started out as a joke, but later we became serious about it. It had a strong effect. In fact, it's still in my head even now. The assemblies were much better without all the 'freshmen suck,' 'sophomores suck' stuff. We really got it bad my freshman year. As time went by, that tradition faded away. We didn't do it when it was our turn, and I didn't regret not having a chance to get even. It was good that it was gone.

"We learned a great deal about understanding different types of people," Chareonchump summarizes. "I learned how to deal with different situations and how to handle myself in a crowd. Plus, I learned that people have a lot of different opinions on moral topics, and it was beneficial to hear how people felt."

Branden Happ, '99, now a Purdue engineering student, was less enthusiastic about First Class—even when considering that it was born out of his sister Megan's unique homecoming crowning. "I didn't enjoy it that much. It was pointless. The worksheets were dumb. They had us write 'three ways to improve the high school' and 'three things that we felt were wrong.' Pointless. Sure, the situation got better, but things change from year to year anyway. There was more respect, but that could be attributed to anything. A lot of seniors didn't even go to the classes. I'm sure other people got a lot out of it. You get out of it what you put into it, and I personally didn't put much in. But I'm sure it had some effect on the school. A lot of my friends were Student Leaders and they were into it, so maybe my perspective is off. I didn't talk much to them about it.

"I didn't want to be a leader myself because I didn't want to take classes in the summer. That was asking too much. Still, I'd recommend the program," the aspiring engineer surprisingly concludes. "Even if it didn't do much, it shortened the other classes and was a break in the day. It was easy, and there wasn't much thinking involved."

Contrasting Happ's blasé view is that of his classmate Mary Ann Ranchero, '99, a bubbly and cheerful young woman of Filipino descent who managed to get herself elected Class President a remarkable three years running, holding power from her sophomore through senior years. Currently brightening the campus at the University of Illinois, Ranchero was naturally highly involved with First Class—and knew how to work it for the benefit of her constituency.

"Throughout 1996-97 the juniors were really upset about what was happening to the school. We sophomores talked about it as well. We'd lost a lot of privileges that we wanted back, especially the Senior Girls Sleepover. So, when it came our turn, we proposed a first-class way of doing it, promising to decorate the school with style, having chaperones, giving out a list of our parents' phone numbers, etc. That way, we were able to get it back. We also fought to get a junior lounge area in the cafeteria and promised to be first class about it, so we gained that as well. We were able to get a lot of things back."

As for the classes themselves, Ranchero's views reflect those of her peers. "Some leaders were effective, and other's weren't. If you were in a class with an ineffective leader, you didn't get much out of it. At the assemblies, we had to sit with our First Class groups instead of our friends and classmates. I hated that! I know the yelling at the freshmen stopped and the students behaved better, but I hated that aspect. I wanted to sit with my class!"

To secure future votes, no doubt.

Despite the assembly bummer, Ranchero felt the program succeeded that initial year in other ways over and above winning back class privileges through persistent persuasion. "It was slowly having a positive effect on the school. I mean, you probably won't get a student to say it was the greatest thing ever, even if they felt that way. Some of it was silly. But it did calm things down. I'm not sure if it was the kids themselves who were responsible for this, or if it was the First Class program. The '98 seniors weren't as rowdy as the '97 seniors.

"In the summer before my senior year, I was picked to be a Student Leader for the second year of First Class. I didn't mind the training classes. It's the kind of thing I do anyway. I was really involved—track, basketball, student government, you name it. At the start of the year, we 'decorated' the school a bit, did the T-paper thing, but we didn't spray graffiti or vandalize. Nobody complained. Then the classes started. The First Class program changed that second year from weekly 20-minute classes to 40 minutes every other week. I think that was better because it gave us more time to discuss things. It was different overall the second year. The first year most of us thought it was silly and foolish. The second year, the students began to open up more to what we were trying to accomplish. But we still had problems. One boy purposely pretended to sleep right in front of me. I handled it by calling on him all the time. He had to stay alert! As the year progressed, the students became more involved. The time would fly by if we had a good discussion going. Even the troublemakers would get into it."

Ranchero believes that one area where the First Class program excelled was in identifying students who might be going through some severe personal difficulties—like the two boys at Columbine.

"They could have vented their anger in First Class. It would have been an outlet for them. Then again, a lot of the athletes and popular kids were student leaders, and that was their problem, so you never know. Overall, I think it would have helped. If Dylan and Eric were in my First Class, I would have gotten to know them. I would have talked to them. I wanted to know who everybody was, so there would have been personal contact. I would have asked them why they were so upset and angry, and let them get it out. Then, if I saw that it wasn't helping, that their anger was building instead of decreasing, I would have taken it to a teacher for advice. The school might have been able to step in and do something professionally to help them.

"Then again, outcasts usually don't have respect for students like me, so it's hard to say. I still think it would have helped. As silly as it might sound, it could have changed everything. It's the little things that people do that make a difference. To have First Class every week, or every other week, they might not have been so mad. That might have been all it took. Just someone to listen to them."

Looking back, Ranchero said she wished she had used the First Class concept to resolve a conflict that she had with her basketball coach. "I was taking violin lessons my junior year on the same days as some of our games. The lessons were usually at 10 A.M. and the games were at 1 P.M. The senior point guard was hurt, so I was scheduled to start. I was a little late, a minute or so, and the coach jumped all over me. He was all pissed off and benched me. That was his style, to bench people for whatever reason. He never did let me play, so my senior year, I didn't go out for the team. I regret that now because I say to myself, 'I should have played basketball that year! I would have enjoyed my senior year more.' I never talked to him about it. We didn't communicate. I just didn't think to go do it. I'm not sure why. I had a lot on my plate and let it slide. Looking back, I realize I didn't implement the First Class ideals there. I should have worked it out with him.

"Am I a better person because of First Class? I would say yes, because, overall, it's good in the long run. But I was a good person to begin with!"

Ranchero's long-time boyfriend, Jeff Czarnota, '99, naturally agrees with her self-assessment. However, Czarnota, now a Western Michigan business student, saw a marked difference between Mundelein and the high school he attended, Adlai Stevenson in nearby Lincolnsville, Illinois.

"I don't think Mary Ann changed because of First Class. I've known her since sixth grade, and she's always the same. She always had good values. I wouldn't want her to change. But Mundelein, that was different. I thought the atmosphere at her school changed for the better. First Class made the younger students feel more comfortable. They had less to fear. The older students at Mundelein weren't so mean to them. I would recommend First Class. It built character, and the student instructors got a lot out of it. They were able to relate their own experiences."

Despite that glowing endorsement from an outsider looking in, Brian McSweeney, '99, was a Mundelein student who was definitely an insider looking to get out—which he did the hard way.

"I liked it the old way before First Class," he reminisces. "When I was a freshman, the whole school screamed, 'freshmen suck' at us and we took it like a man. Then, after First Class, they stopped it. It might sound stupid, but I was bummed. We never had our chance to shine. My sister was chased by the police for spray painting the school her senior year. I didn't get to do that either.

"What I remember about First Class is a lot of people ditched it, including myself. The problem was there was no grade. They took attendance, but that was it. The period after First Class was lunch, so by ditching it, I had a nice long lunch. I wasn't a bad kid. I got good grades. I was on the homecoming court, played hockey and some basketball. I just liked the looser atmosphere we had before. It seemed like the First Class kids put a lot of rules on themselves. We weren't able to TP the school, and they took the Senior Girls Sleepover away so there were no bras and panties hanging from the windows the next morning for the freshmen to see. In exchange, there were ID cards and hall monitors.

"I went to a few of the classes my junior year. We talked about how to be nice to each other. I didn't feel it pertained to me in the least. I was in the high school zone, doing whatever I was doing and First Class was getting in the way. There was a gigantic change in the way the school was run. There were more restrictions. When I was a freshman I could go off campus for lunch five times a week! My junior year, we could go only twice a week. We were reverting! I'm sure the school overall was a better place, but not for me. It was like being able to drive a Lamborghini to school my freshman year, then having to go in a beat-up '82 Datsun my junior year. It was just a lot more fun before First Class.

"When I was a senior, a group of us were going to decorate the school again, like in the old days. We came around 8 A.M., about seven trucks of us party types, armed with shaving cream, toilet paper, eggs, etc. When we arrived, the principal was there and cops were everywhere! What kind of fun is that? They said they wanted to make sure we were 'tasteful.' So we did a few things, chalk writing, some toilet papering, but we didn't have the same enthusiasm with the police and administration staring at us. Then after we left, they cleaned most of it up before anyone saw it.   •

"I had an early-bird class at 6 A.M. that year that was hard to wake up for. I was usually partying all night, so that made it especially difficult. I kept getting unexcused absences from my morning classes, and skipped almost all of First Class. I didn't see the importance of it.

"Looking back on Mundelein, I'd say it's a lot better. I wasn't a fan of First Class, but then again, I was acting pretty stupid. I can see that something needed to happen to turn things around. Each class was trying to outdo the other in trashing the place, and it was getting wild. Fun, but wild. Guess that had to stop. If it had to happen during my years, so be it. The freshmen today don't know the way it was."

To balance that colorful venture into the fringes of the high school Twilight Zone, an update from freshman First Class pioneer Jennifer Bouteille is warranted. Bouteille, as mentioned in Chapter 2, was in the unique position of having been in on the original, point-zero planning of First Class with the founding juniors. However, unlike them, she had enough time left to watch it progress through three years.

"I went through the summer training program my junior year when we changed it so that underclassmen could be Student Leaders," she begins. "It's like everybody said, playing games that taught us how to work together and get people involved, how to call on them and engage the students in topics they enjoyed. If there was a bad topic that wasn't working, we were told to ask them what they wanted to talk about. We were also told to take notes on what worked and report back to Ms. Royer and Coach Ahlgrim.

"I'm a vocal person, so I liked being a leader. I enjoyed the challenge of getting the students involved and accomplishing goals. There was a big change in the school that first year when First Class started, and I wanted to continue it. A lot of students in 1997-98 thought it was childish and foolish, and they didn't want to talk, so our goal was to bring them out of their shells. And it was important to remind them that we ourselves decided that we needed to settle down. It was not something the teachers were forcing on us.

"My senior year, I became an M-Team member. I went through additional problem-solving training that summer. That was another challenge, to be able to go into a room where I didn't know anybody and get a discussion going. I liked that. We were also called in if a class leader was having difficulties with a kid, or a group of kids who weren't behaving. We'd go in there and double team them, find out what the troublemakers were into, and try to get them engaged. If they continued to goof around, we would say 'okay, seriously, you need to stop.' They would.

"There was a tremendous difference in the school between my freshman and senior years. It became so much better. There was no name calling anymore, and hardly any fights. My freshman year, there were so many fights. I must have seen 10 myself! My senior year, I can remember only one fight. There was a lot less tension. Classes were more interactive, not just First Class, but all the classes. The upperclassmen didn't ignore the underclassmen and treat them like they didn't exist. It was fun to see what we started in Ms. Royer's French class in 1996 grow like that. There was respect, and you could feel it all over. And each year got better. We lived through it, the bad times that started it and the corrections that came out of it. First Class became a tradition.

"Personally, I became a better person because of it. When you were a Student Leader, or M-Team member, all eyes were on you all day long, so you had to set an example. You couldn't let your guard down. It also helped me to be concerned with the feelings of others, and to know how stupid it is to make fun of people. I find myself to this day biting my tongue and thinking, 'Don't say that. That's not first class.'

"I think First Class would have prevented what happened at Columbine. One year, I had the top Goth in my First Class. This is a group that dresses in black, gothic clothes, trench coats, chains, and spiked collars. They were similar to the ones at Columbine. This Goth in my class, she really participated. She always seemed to take the opposing view on an issue, but she and her gang talked and took part. I had another Goth in a different First Class and he was talkative as well. He usually took the opposite view of everyone else. We'd be talking about manners, and the need to be nice and respect each other, and he'd pipe up and say, 'Hey, the world isn't Barney and Mr. Rogers. Not everybody out there is going to say *please* and *thank you.*' So they brought that side to the table, and it was fascinating to get their perspective on things, even if it was different.

"I didn't notice anybody else on the edge other than the Goths, and the Goths would talk freely about sensitive, personal topics, so I gained respect for them. I saw them as people, not black gothic clothes, chains, spikes and funny hair.

"I think First Class would have spent Dylan and Eric's rage. We covered so many topics over the years, something would have opened them up. These kinds of people usually want to be listened to. They like to talk and give their views. The problem is when they don't have an outlet, no one listens. First Class would have given them the opportunity to be heard."

What emerges from this first set of student reactions is that those who experienced the initial, dramatic transformation have a stronger opinion about the positives of character education than those who came later and never lived through the chaos that spawned the movement. This follows the normal evolution of any corrective measure. Years before, the Deerfield High administrators experienced this same phenomena and concluded that complacency was something they would have to constantly battle. By the third year, Mundelein was already beginning to face this creeping contentment as well. The teachers, Student Leaders, and administrators had to evaluate whether it was time to phase out the Character Education program because the "disease" of bad behavior had been cured, or to keep it going strong to prevent the illness from returning. The directive to continue pushing hard came, once again, from setting everything aside and listening closely to the often contradictory opinions of the students themselves—both the goody two-shoes and the rebels without a cause.

Graham Beatty, 2001, was indoctrinated with the First Class program from the moment he entered the now calm, well-behaved school. As Brian McSweeney would say, he never knew what he had missed, or was missing. Not surprisingly, his views are mixed. Like many students who came later, he sees both the good and the bad.

"I pretty much didn't like it. My freshman year I thought First Class was silly. It didn't seem to be very efficient. I didn't see it as a good catalyst for teaching values the way it was set up with the ice breakers and stuff. Everybody has an attitude in the beginning. 'This is dumb.' Same thing every year. A couple of kids would sit and do their homework. But everyone eventually was worked in. As the year went on, the whole class usually got into the discussions. We discussed real hard issues like alcohol, and looked at it from different perspectives. It was better in the following years because the topics and lesson plans weren't all centered upon self-esteem and using bad words. There were more real-life issues. But even then, it got repetitive and lost its momentum. We kept going back to the same issues like racism. In general, it seemed childish. A lot of students thought they were too cool for it. They'd sit there and not participate. It was different from class to class. Sometimes the teacher took over. Sometimes the kids did it all.

"I supported the concept of what they were trying to accomplish. But they needed to make sure the goals are the same for each group, which I saw as 'pride in the school' and 'acting first class.' They were getting away from that and going off on other tangents. I think the main goal of the program was getting lost."

Despite Beatty's less-than-stellar support, the six-foot, five-inch basketball player was nonetheless drafted to become a Student Leader his junior year. "I accepted it. I wanted to help out, plus all the cool kids were picked. I had a good group of kids in my class, so it worked well. My personal goal was to make do and get everybody involved. It was still too random and not step-by-step for me. Plus, that was the first year they changed to every other week and that was bad. The momentum as lost. You couldn't bond by skipping a week.

"I didn't notice a change in the school because of it. It was not incredibly effective. It didn't turn the school around. It just gave some people extra time to do their homework."

Again, it's critical to point out that Beatty arrived at Mundelein after the First Class program had made giant inroads in blotting out the misadventures that had plagued the campus during his spirited sister Blaire's heyday in '96 and '97. Those wild years became a fading, if not completely forgotten memory as each new group of bright-eyed freshmen took their seats and pushed out another graduating class. With little left to form a reference point, it became harder and harder for the new classes to understand the need for such an elaborate Character Education curriculum.

With that said, even the young turks like Beatty were stunned into some degree of awareness by the shocking murders at Columbine in the spring of 1999. Criticisms aside, they almost universally viewed First Class as the perfect place for teenage outcasts on the edge to vent some of their rage. "Instead of being isolated, they would be in a group where they could see people as individuals and understand that everybody has problems, not just them."

It's also interesting to note that while Beatty attended First Class for two years, was a leader his third, and was planning to be a leader again his senior year, he was unaware that the program was originally conceived by students. As the First Class founders had warned, Beatty's lukewarm reaction could have been derived from the fact that he went in with the wrong 'top-down' perspective from the start. "I never heard about how it started. If that's the case, it should be more in tune with our lives."

TJ Waskey, 2000, an Illinois Wesleyan pre-med student, knew a bit more about the origins of First Class from his former Student Leader sister, Julie, and his activist father, Tony. Regardless, he also has divided feelings about his own experience. "Some of the activities were childish and a waste of time. Others were good. Toward my senior year, it was getting better. That's because it was becoming more student run. A lot of people did enjoy the classes. It cut the day shorter, and there was no homework or grades, so the atmosphere was relaxed.

"After Columbine, we spent a lot of time in First Class talking about what happened there. It was good that we had that outlet to discuss it. They also cracked down on the kids at our school (the Goths and trench-coat set) who dressed like that. A good thing about First Class is it showed everybody that they are not alone in how they feel. Everybody was working together with people they wouldn't have ordinarily been working with.

"I think it was worthwhile to have it. There were notable changes in the school. I suspect over the next years it will get even better. The kids won't know anything but First Class, and it won't be the joke some of us thought it was."

Luke Hajzl, '98, is one of the original student leaders that future Mundelein students—and high school students everywhere—need to listen to in order to understand precisely why those often seemingly silly Character Education classes are so important to institute and maintain. While many of the former football captain's successors gripe about First Class, Hajzl, like most of the Mundelein founders, now wishes he would have had the opportunity to experience a few more years of it. And unlike the students populating Mundelein's halls today, he clearly remembers the way it used to be.

"I didn't think the previous seniors back then were that bad, that far out of the ordinary. There was some drinking in the house across the street, and a small number of kids around school were using coke, but it was the usual stuff. However, the students in general didn't have much respect for each other, and a lot of teachers were taking crap from them. Mundelein was the kind of place where if you wanted to learn, you could. If you didn't want to, you could still slide through. I wanted to change that, to see more school pride and a better atmosphere. So, when the movement started, I hopped on board. I signed the petition, attended the open forums, and was chosen to be a Student Leader.

"I ended up with a good group that started right off with a lot of participation. I shared the Student Leader duties with a co-leader, Erin Karzack, and we interacted well together. The family topics went over with the students, stuff like 'Why my parents are ragging on me.' A couple of kids in my class had parents that were real A-holes, so everyone sympathized and shared their own stories. We didn't have much trouble with discipline. The biggest troublemaker in the class was my best friend's brother's little friend, so I could deal with him. He'd make a joke, and I'd let the class laugh, then bring his joke into the discussion. 'Do the rest of you agree with that?' I'd ask. I had a little trouble with this Mexican girl who had an attitude. She was the typical, head-shaking Jerry Springer type who wore five tons of makeup and thought she was tough. I diffused most of her attitude because I speak Spanish. I could understand what she and her crew were saying to each other in private. When they'd make a crack in Spanish, I'd translate it to the entire class. That embarrassed her, so she quit. Of course, she didn't show up much anyway. That was the main discipline problem—getting people to show up. We had three or four out of the 16 who never appeared."

Luke's classmate, Gwen Stepan, '98, was a varsity gymnast and volleyball player who, for reasons that still baffle her, was not among the 100-plus incoming seniors selected to be a Student Leader during the kick-off year. Despite that slight, she is positive about the experience and reiterates that it's important for today's students to be told about the program's "bottom-up" roots. "I always wondered why I wasn't asked to be a Student Leader, but never received an answer. I did go to the classes. It was neat the way they had four students from each year there. That enabled us to get to know other students in the school. I think it works well that way. When I was a freshman, it was 'Oh, those big, scary seniors!'

"It was nice to have a class taught by students, not by teachers. You tend to listen more, and have fun. I personally thought we needed to have greater respect for the school. Since it was students saying that we should change our behavior and maturity, that hit us harder. It was better that way. As we get older, we're supposed to have less and less rules, but here we were putting more on ourselves. In the long run, it felt much better even if it was hard to adapt to losing some privileges. The freshmen and sophomores coming in carried on the respect for the school and the teachers, and toned down the language they were using. A lot of kids before had no idea how to treat people with respect.

"I think those guys at Columbine were too secluded. If they had a program like this they wouldn't have killed all those kids. They would have had more interaction with students across class lines, so that kind of reaction could have been avoided. They could have talked out their problems in First Class.

"I really would recommend this for other schools. It's tough to get started and hard in those initial classes, but in the long term it's beneficial. I wish I'd had it from my freshman year on. Maybe I'd have been a better person."

Despite such endorsements, there are always going to be those who simply won't go with the flow. And they aren't just the malcontents, nor are they limited to those who "didn't know how bad it was before." Like her friend Mary Ann Ranchero, Marit Johnson, '99, was heavily involved in student government. Unlike Ranchero, however, she prefers that traditional form of student leadership over the new-fangled Character Education curriculums.

"The First Class program was obviously created with good intentions, but I personally don't believe it had any significant impact while I was in school. Of course, I'm speaking through my own experience, and I had the trial run of it because it was a new program when I was at Mundelein. The lessons involved in the classes had good content to them, but the activities that we were instructed to do as a follow-up to the lessons were sometimes a little juvenile. I enjoyed when we watched clips of movies or news shows that pertained to the subject being discussed, because then I could see the issue in real life. That was a reality check for students because it enabled them to see how their individual problems were plaguing society as a whole. I also enjoyed the class discussions. Of course, that was only fun when people participated instead of just speaking when called on.

"I felt that the program was a start to a long struggle of trying to regain respect and standards in our school. Unfortunately, many of the students would bad talk it and completely make fun of it. So there was definitely a negative attitude. With this attitude, nothing will ever be improved. I'm not bashing the program because I, too, believe that an action had to be taken to help increase respect, especially among teenagers, but there is always room for improvements. The decline of morals and values is a huge problem in today's world, and if high schools can do something to help change that, then I say 'go for it.'"

Steve Wheeler, '99, is of the "bad talk," Brian McSweeney school of diminishing extracurricular experiences. He offered his frank views as former "Alice in Chains" guitarist Jerry Cantrell wailed on the CD player in the background. "I thought First Class was a complete waste of time. No one liked it except the Student Leaders, and most of them didn't like it either. They just did it for their college transcripts. I'd say 85 percent of the kids didn't like it. We talked about the same things all year. Don't drink and drive, don't be a racist, treat people how you want to be treated, and sexual harassment. We spent months on sexual harassment. It was all obvious stuff I've heard since grammar school. Nothing new.

"Should Mundelein scrap First Class? That's really tough to say. They put three years into it. I wouldn't scrap it, but I'd try to make it more student oriented. Let the students pick the topics, not the teachers and Student Leaders. And I'd get rid of those stupid movies and videos they show us. There was one about underage drinking that was shot in the 1970s. The hair and clothes just made us laugh, and it was poorly done and unreal, way stretched. They had kids downing huge amounts of alcohol and then going drag racing and stuff like that. It looked so phony. The sexual harassment film was more recent, early '90s, but they went way overboard in determining what was considered sexual harassment. Every little joke or typical teenage statement they included as sexual harassment. It was stupid. But at least they weren't wearing disco clothes from the 1970s."

TJ Waskey's older sister, Julie, another member of the founding leadership class of '98, cringes at such sentiments. Even though she only experienced that first dramatic year, she is more positive about it than her younger brother, and far more positive than Wheeler and McSweeney.

"I didn't think the program changed things. I think the *kids* changed things. The classes before us were so bad. I don't think we'd have caused those kind of problems either way, even without First Class. But going through it was good. I liked the fact that if you were caught doing something bad, the First Class way of handling it was to erase it by doing something good. Say you cursed at someone and got caught. Instead of being punished, you could compliment someone, be positive about something, show some school spirit.

"The biggest change I saw was that the school was more interactive, more mixed than before. You'd see freshmen interacting with juniors and seniors. Some even started hanging out together. You never saw anything like that before."

Waskey said there's a lot about First Class that she plans to carry with her into her future profession as an elementary school teacher, and a lot that she won't be able to because of the different dynamics between elementary and high school.

"You don't have the same problems. Elementary students aren't getting drunk during lunch and trashing the school. At that age, students are teacher pleasers, not peer pleasers. It's not until around the fifth grade that they start becoming peer or friend pleasers. That's when they don't care what the teacher thinks, they want to show off for their friends. In elementary school, you can't really compliment a student too much either because they will get branded as a teacher's pet. You can't discipline them in a way that embarrasses them in front of their classmates because their egos are so fragile. So a lot of the First Class program topics and roll playing wouldn't carry over to the younger classes."

Even so, it's comforting to think that former Mundelein First Class graduates like Julie Waskey are out there in colleges and universities today, working toward becoming teachers themselves. That means what they went through during those turbulent years at Mundelein, and the bottom-up movement they started, will live on through the next generation.

As for the student naysayers, the ground-level perspective from those in the heart of the grinder is no doubt worthwhile, as it tends to be more emotionally charged and intense. With that said, it is by no means the only perspective that carries weight. Sometimes, those a step or two removed from center of a whirlwind can look upon what's going on without the emotion and attitude, and with wider, more encompassing eyes. From this angle, the picture of the First Class program crystallizes even further.

CHAPTER 7

PARENTS, TEACHERS, AND
ADMINISTRATORS REACT

While Mundelein's fickle student body may have had mixed feelings about the First Class program, the bar shoots dramatically skyward when considering the reactions of the parents, teachers, and administrators. So much so, in fact, there's hardly a hedged bet anywhere.

Kelly Happ, mother of the infamous '97 homecoming queen Megan and her ambivalent brother Branden, '99, is a First Class supporter all the way. This carries a lot of weight because Happ, the appalled parent who watched in tears as a homecoming queen selection spiraled out of control, is now sitting on the local school board.

"I've seen a difference at Mundelein, a big difference, since the First Class program was instituted," Happ says, noting that she had two previous children, Dorrie, '93, and Chris, '95, attend Mundelein as well. "There's a nicer, friendlier atmosphere at the school. The assemblies are more polite, more respectful, and the students are careful about their language. I think First Class has created an awareness in the students to respect others as individuals, and that attitude seems to have grown with each year.

"As far as I'm aware, it was never an issue with the previous school board. It was a nonissue in terms of objections. People are happy with it. We now have an advisory program that meets a couple of times a month to discuss the topics they are using. That helps keep everyone in the community involved.

"I would highly recommend it to other schools and districts. I visited a fifth-grade class that had a version of it in operation where the students were asked to make five positive comments about their school. They stood straight and said them with sure voices. I was so impressed! I'd like to see it catch on all over the country. First Class is the antidote to Columbine."

Mary Ann Beatty, mother of the theatrical Blaire, '97, the sedate Graham, 2000, and their predecessor, Maureen, '95, is another solid supporter. A big reason is that she doubles as a Latin and voice teacher at nearby Deerfield High—the place where the administrative-driven First Class movement originated.

"I have to say I like the program. It's about issues that affect students' lives that they can discuss without being hassled. Before First Class, the students didn't have an effective avenue for discussion. And sometimes their energies were misapplied, especially around homecoming. I remember one year they planted a tree right on the football field! The students needed to learn that it wasn't just about vandalizing their school; it was about showing respect for the entire community. We've had First Class at Deerfield for 10 years now and, as a result, there is a real closeness among the kids, faculty, staff, and even the cafeteria workers. You really get the feeling that they are family. If that's because of First Class, then I'm all for it!

"I realize that on the classroom level, it's only as effective as the peer leader. And in other classes, some kids don't buy into it, but overall, you can see the change it's made. My son Graham's been through the Mundelein First Class program for three years now. He comes from a 'talky' family. We discuss all the issues in our home, you name it, so that was nothing new for him. He was always a good kid.

"It takes a while for the behavioral changes to set in. I didn't see major changes overnight. The teachers and kids have to buy into it. If you have one faculty member who doesn't, a person who thinks it's a drag, or it's not part of their job, or displays a bad attitude about it, then it blows the whole program. The word spreads that not everyone is with it, and the students pick up on it."

Teacher buy-in is an area where a 'top-down' initiative does have its benefits. They were able to more easily overcome the influence of negative teachers at Deerfield because First Class was the creation, and pet project, of their charismatic principal, John Scornavacco. "It's more accepted and expanded at Deerfield," Beatty confirms. "There are all kinds of other activities associated with it there. I think you need five years to judge a program's effect, and Mundelein hasn't hit that yet. Deerfield has a full week of First Class–related activities and assemblies that raise amazing amounts of money for handicapped kids. I think we passed $25,000 last year. There's a barbecue in the courtyard, and both student and faculty rock bands perform. It's a real caring atmosphere, one that takes a while to build. You couldn't have a barbecue at a school where the kids will end up throwing hot coals at each other. I think Mundelein will reach the point where Deerfield is today. I don't know the time frame, but they'll get there. I really believe in dialogue and refinement. The First Class program should be scrutinized each year to make it better."

Some of the Mundelein parents and teachers are already doing their own part to "make it better." As a corollary activity related to the principles of First Class, a parent/teacher group started an outreach program into the Hispanic neighborhoods. "The Hispanics make up about 21 percent of Mundelein, so it's important to make them feel included," Beatty explains. "There's a language and cultural barrier there that must be overcome. They've had some talented students from that community who were offered college scholarships, and their parents rejected them because they wanted their children to remain closer to home. We would visit them and try to convince them how important it is for their child, and their community, to allow them to attend the distant colleges. In doing that, we've been able to convince many of the kids and their parents to accept the scholarships."

Beatty shares the view expressed by the Mundelein students that a First Class program can identify and turn around the antisocial behavior of misfits and loaners who are building up to an emotional meltdown.

"I think it could have made a difference at places like Columbine, because First Class specifically creates an atmosphere of acceptance.

If First Class had been established at Columbine and had been successful for at least three years—with the right kind of faculty/student leadership, program direction, and evaluation, along with the adoption of the concept by the majority of the school population—perhaps Eric and Dylan would have felt comfortable and accepted enough to have shared their feelings. But the parents need to play a role as well. Would I have known something like that (building pipe bombs) was going on in my kid's room? I'm no snoop, but I'd have known. We don't mince words around our house. If I saw something odd going on, I'd have confronted my children.

"With a First Class program in place, it would have come out that the fringe groups were being harassed. You could take the time, maybe spend a month on the topic. Feelings would have emerged. The students could have expressed what they were going through. This is why I feel getting the counselors more involved needs to have a higher profile in First Class. Not during the initial year of the program, but later on in the following years. Some kids have no community other than their school. There is no parent component in some of these families. They are getting what they get in school, and on the Internet.

"I would recommend First Class to other schools, but it needs to be tailored to their own community and customized for each campus. There also needs to be a caring about the school community. The students should feel they have something worth caring about during four critical years of their lives. First Class teaches them that what they say or do affects the whole community."

Maggie Johnson, mother of Andy, '96, and politically minded Marit, '99, is another person who has seen both sides of the Mundelein coin—the good years and bad. And she did so from the duel perspective of a parent and a jack-of-all-subjects substitute teacher. Johnson has mixed feelings about First Class. "I thought the idea and concept was really good. It was great they were trying to do something like that. As a school grows and becomes larger, you lose community rather than gain it. It was becoming a trend for the students to knock down the other grades at assemblies. It's an awful thing to have huge rivalries like that inside a school.

"The best part of First Class was that it was a kid, Bill Zasadil, who got it started. And he wasn't a nerd. He was the quarterback, a macho guy who the other students' respected. I don't think it would have been accepted if it was just another thing started by the staff to try to get the students to behave. On the down side, it was a burgeoning program and I don't feel they selected the subjects well or presented them effectively. Plus, they didn't have the cooperation of all the teachers right away. There were moans and groans. Some said things like 'Come on, you're making us do something else?' I think it goes back to not embracing the teachers from the beginning. You can have Student Leaders running it, but you still need the faculty to give their support.

"My daughter Marit, who was active in student government, really didn't embrace it either. Some kids simply don't think it's cool. They think it's kind of dorky. Many don't show up. Others just cross their arms and sit there with disgusted looks on their faces and refuse to participate. But it differs from class to class. I subbed just recently and the Student Leader, Chris Lepley, did a pretty good job. Nobody was negative. They did the exercise of writing three things about themselves, two of which were true and one that was false (and the rest would have to guess which was which). That worked out well.

"I think Mundelein has experienced better moments because of First Class. Even though the kids half make fun of it, you do hear them say, 'That's not very first class.' So a lot of it is sinking in."

Sharon Zasadil, mother of non-nerd Bill, the BMOC student usually given the most credit for leading the character education charge at Mundelein, said she knew he was unhappy with the school in his early years. "We had a lot of discussions about the apathy at Mundelein, and the frequent fights. There was a large Hispanic population and the lines had been drawn culturally. I used to tell Bill that he could outfight anybody with his mouth, not his fists. Aside from that, everyone seemed to be abusing the school, and it was just negative, negative, negative. There was trash all over the cafeteria, graffiti on the walls and sidewalks, and absolutely no school spirit. The attendance at the sporting events was next to nothing. I'd hear Bill and his friends talking, and I'd say 'you're always complaining, but you're not doing anything about it.' I knew if anybody could do something, it was Bill and his gang because they were such an amazing group. Even back before high school, you could see there was something special about them. They were so well-rounded and mature, and were always involved in doing positive things. There were about 15 of them, and as they grew up, they became committed to what they wanted to accomplish. They were the kind of kids that got things done.

"When I began to hear about what they were trying to do, I knew right off that Bill would be one of the main leaders. He always had a very strong sense of self and purpose, even if, at times, he marched to his own drum. His friend, Luke Hajzl, was so charismatic, I suspected that he would emerge as a leader as well. It's not hard to see how the other students followed them. It didn't surprise me how they were able to turn the school around.

"By Bill's senior year, there was such a remarkable difference at Mundelein. You had to go early to the football and basketball games or you wouldn't be able to find a seat! The homecoming parade was lined with beautiful floats. The support and spirit of the student body was tremendous. At the same time, I stopped hearing about fights in the lunchroom, cultural tensions, trash, vandalism, and things like that.

"I was so proud to see that they had done something about the problems instead of just sitting around and complaining. Bill put his money where his mouth was, which didn't surprise me because he was always that type of person."

Tony Waskey, father of squeaky-clean Julie, '98, and TJ, 2000, is an outspoken parent who enjoyed having first-hand involvement with all aspects of his children's education.

"We were somewhat aware of the problems they were having in 1996-97. I assumed it was the typical upper classes making the underclasses pay their dues. We were distanced because my kids didn't hang out with the problem crowd. Julie hung out with the Eagle Scouts and Boy Scouts. TJ came to me one day and broke down and said, 'You don't know what it's like to be me.' Apparently his old friends from grade school and junior high had started drinking and smoking and going wild, and he had to get away from them because he wasn't into that. Fortunately for us, he had a good head on his shoulders."

The senior Waskey gives Principal John Davis credit for melding the student body and trying to end the heated class rivalries, although he admits he wasn't quite sold in the beginning.

"John Davis started to blend in and tone down and do away with class groupings, including the separation between the smart and not so smart. Some of us parents were against that last one. I think you should reward those who excel. Davis wanted to blend and mellow the student body, which I thought was good in general later on. First Class did the bonding and mentoring. TJ was required to tutor (student lead) other students. They brought in a mixture of classes so he could get involved with different kids than he normally would have and helped them with an attitude adjustment.

"Julie was very proud to be part of that initial group of leaders, and was proud of the class that she mentored. The kids felt she was a first-class leader. She didn't explain the details to me, but we know that it helped her self-esteem. She was able to recognize problems and figure out how to solve them.

"The assemblies have been improving. I've been going to graduation for years. It was kind of lame in the past because Davis had to talk down to the students and keep reminding them to behave. They usually didn't. They'd act bored and start taking off their gowns before it was over. When Julie was in the tenth grade (1996-97) even in the National Honor Society assembly the kids would chatter, move around, and disrupt the proceedings. They had no respect for the speaker. More recently, things have changed. Davis hasn't had to make those announcements about the students behaving. There appears to be a lot more self-discipline among the students."

Founding teacher Karen Royer agrees, expressing elation and pride over the way the program she helped create and institute, at great professional risk, ended up playing out in the reality of the *Blackboard Jungle**.

"I remember one discussion that was so involved and lively it summed up everything good about First Class. There was a news item about a man who raped and murdered a young girl in the bathroom of a Las Vegas casino. What people don't remember is that he had a friend who, although he didn't participate, stood by and allowed it to happen. That led to a discussion about right and wrong versus loyalty

---

Blackboard Jungle is a seminal, 1950s high school melodrama that starred Glenn Ford as a harried teacher trying to get through to his "hooligan" students who were angry and scarred by life in a tough, low-income neighborhood. Released in 1955, it also starred Sidney Poitier, Anne Francis, and Vic Morrow, and is most remembered for its then novel rock-and-roll soundtrack, which included the classic song "Rock Around the Clock." The film, while no critic's darling at the time, set the formula for scores of high school films that have followed to this day. Poitier himself went on to make a similar film, *To Sir with Love,* which was about an American teacher trying to get through to English hooligans from a similarly depressed background.

to friends, which is a critical issue on the high school level. Even with the extreme example, there was a reluctance among many to squeal on a friend. When the example wasn't so extreme, it was an even tougher call. The conversation that day spilled out into the hallways, into their next classes, and was continued in First Class a week later.

"What I also enjoyed was seeing how the Student Leaders grew into their leadership roles, and how their classes changed as a result of it. Classes that started off with problems developed into wonderful experiences as the leaders learned and matured. At the same time, you could see the Student Leaders' enthusiasm and sense of self-worth expand. The big issue on a personal level remained the concept of self-reflection: 'Where are we going from here?'; 'How will this affect our lives beyond school?'; 'What will we take with us as human beings?' The tendency was to initially choose leaders who were involved in everything else at school. They agreed to go along with this out of the goodness of their hearts, even if they were ambivalent about it. On top of everything else, sports, extracurricular activities, clubs, etc., they met at 7 A.M. on Monday mornings during the school year to prepare the lessons. Seeing this kind of extraordinary effort made the faculty feel better about it.

"As dramatic as the changes the first year were, the transformation between the first and second years was also important. The students were proud of their success, and success begets success. Clean halls, good behavior, better language, that became 'the way it is.' The First Class way became *the* way. It was such a joy to walk down the hall and not hear a single 'F-you' being said anywhere. There were so many similar side effects that were just wonderful to experience.

"When we heard about the Columbine shootings, we immediately canceled our routine schedule and sent the students to their First Class rooms. We talked about what happened, and whether they felt safe at school. We listened to their concerns, and asked them what they thought we as a school could do to prevent such outbursts. It also helped us explain that the ID policy we had in effect wasn't a nuisance, but was there to keep out outsiders who might want to hurt them. We were able to make it clear that the rules and regulations were not created to annoy them, but to protect them. We weren't trying to clutter up their lives with moral issues; we were trying to keep them safe. Columbine presented an opportunity not only to discuss the rules, but to talk about clothing and appearance choices. That went both ways because I remember that hooded sweatshirts were in fashion that year, and the students wanted us to lighten up on that and let it go. So they were listening to us, and we were listening to them. That's what it's all about.

"We also discussed how First Class would have allowed such enraged students to vent their anger, and that they would have been able to do so starting as freshmen. We reiterated how important it was to listen to those who have a different way of thinking or looking at things.

"It's nice to think that First Class would have prevented what happened at Columbine, but maybe that's just pie-in-the-sky. How can you ever say definitively that it would have stopped it? But it may have enabled us to identify those with severe problems and get them proper help before they acted upon it. We experienced a number of dramatic personal changes as a result of First Class. We've had many students who went from troublemakers and burn-outs to First Class Student Leaders. They felt that those like themselves wouldn't listen to a cheerleader, so they stepped forward in order to reach their own. That was great! We had many more from all the groups, even the fringe groups, who were against First Class and thought it was a joke then changed their attitudes by their junior or senior years and offered positive testimonies about the experience. Others learned the simple concept that rules aren't made to be broken."

Coach Ahlgrim acted as a troubleshooter that initial semester, monitoring the classes and handling those who were having a more difficult time adapting to Royer's twist on the ol' rules cliché. Even though the football coach was once again playing the role of the heavy, he found the job less taxing than some of his peers had predicted. "We received immediate positive feedback. The opening day assembly went without a hitch and gave us an emotional boost right out of the gate. The students listened attentively to the guest speaker, and had transformed themselves almost overnight into a very respectful, unified community. A lot of the problems we experienced in the past surrounding the assemblies were de-emphasized.

"Realistically, we knew we were dealing with something never tried before. We knew that it would take time for the First Class groups to build a sense of trust. Some Student Leaders were doing an outstanding job, while others needed more time to get the hang of it. Some lessons went well, while others flopped. As a whole, there was a general feeling that even on problem days, that was okay. Not every lesson was going to hit a home run. It was all about the effort. And the teachers were so positive in how they interacted with the Student Leaders. They wanted them to succeed and did everything they could to support them.

"Something else I noticed was the way the First Class Leaders acted the rest of the day. Being a leader heightened the awareness that they were being watched. They realized they had more responsibility to set an example, and you could see them stepping up to another level. They exhibited more initiative, assertiveness, and self-pride. They were paying increased attention to details, better understanding what was important, and seemed to be more aware of everything going on around them. I could even see it on the football field. Because they were First Class Leaders, our team leaders Bill Zasadil and Luke Hajzl were much more willing to tell their peers that something wasn't right, and to do something about it. For me, it was like having an extra staff of coaches out there. Before First Class, Bill and Luke were good leaders. After First Class, they were great leaders. Looking back on the nearly two decades I've coached, when I think of memorable team leaders, those two come to mind."

That's a powerful compliment—but not surprising when considering that Bill was instrumental in conceiving and creating the First Class program at Mundelein, and Luke jumped on board early to help push it along.

"One of the things we stressed in succeeding years was building the confidence and skills of the Student Leaders," Ahlgrim continues. "It was a huge task, for them as well as us. I can't say enough about how important they are to the program. They're constantly fighting peer pressure, and their own internal desire to bail out when things aren't going well. They must constantly receive special handling.

"For all the kids, First Class made them realize that their little world here at Mundelein reflects exactly what they will face in the bigger world later. They learned the positives and negatives of behavior, how to deal with tragedy, how to handle their emotions, and how to improve the climate and culture of their environment.

"Two years ago, a rival school, Libertyville, instituted their First Class program. As part of it, they invited our students to attend a dance with them after the big basketball game. It was a risk because emotions can be high during those rivalries, and that night after the game, one school would be up and the other down, so there was some potential for tension. However, thanks to the First Class programs, it all went well. And during the dance, many of our teachers met with their teachers to discuss how the First Class program was going at each of our schools.

"The following year, it was our turn to host the game. I was still wary of the dance, and the fact that the losing team's students would be low, so we thought of doing something during the game when the emotions of both crowds would still be high. We decided to give out free popcorn. Well, that grew to free pop when a local distributor got word of it, and then free hot dogs when a grocery store stepped up. On the night of the event, we just gave it all away. 'Welcome to a First Class game,' we said, handing everybody the food and drink. We were able to provide as much as they could handle, because we had so much we didn't run out. That put everybody in a good mood. How many times can you go to a sporting event with free, all-you-can-eat concessions? People kept asking us what we were doing, and why, and we said it was because we're being 'first class.' But boy, it was a lot of work! Cooking, preparing the food, serving it, and washing all the pots afterward. My secretary, Diane Risdon, did a tremendous job putting it all together and helping with the 'dirty work.' She was getting nothing out of it, either, and she didn't hesitate to lend a hand. That's what the First Class program does. It makes everybody happy to be involved."

Veteran teacher Dave Ekstrom, a member of the task force that developed the First Class curriculum, had signed up semireluctantly in order to cash in on the stipend that was offered. The Mundelein boys and girls soccer coach ended up becoming a big fan.

"We were all learning as we went along. The more we transferred responsibility to the kids, and took the burden from the teachers, the better it seemed to work. The students needed to have ownership of the program to make it successful. In turn, we had to train them better to do so. In the beginning, they'd glance at the lesson plans right before class and try to wing it. That rarely worked. We later instituted mandatory weekly meetings with the Student Leaders to go over the lessons first. That made a major difference. The first year, I had to step in all the time to keep it going. More recently, I had a strong Student Leader who was always prepared, so I hardly said a word the entire year.

"At the end of the first semester of year one, we had a big party in the gym with free pop, popcorn, and music. We celebrated the effort everyone had put into the program, and the changes that were already apparent in their behavior. Then, near the end of the year, I had the idea of getting them all out on the football field to spell out 'MHS—FIRST CLASS' with their bodies. Math teacher Brian Swanson worked out the placement, and Jim Jackson, our nationally awarded technology teacher, flew over and took a picture in an airplane he and his students had built in his high-tech Aviation class. That was some day!"

Coach Ahlgrim vividly remembers that event as well. "After Brian Swanson drew up the grid from a computer design, basketball coach Terry Wilhelm and I stuck paper on the ground representing each First Class group—all 94—and then began herding the cattle into place. I was amazed how everyone went along with it so well. It had been raining the days before, and I was worried about damaging the field. The sun came out and everything went fine. Science teacher Jack Pawlowski actually took the photograph while Jim Jackson flew the plane. We were in radio contact with them from the ground. They flew over a couple of times to take the shots. The kids didn't really know much about how it looked. They couldn't tell from where they stood. Even from the press box we couldn't see it. We weren't sure how it was going to come out. We were just having fun. When we saw the picture—wow! It came out perfectly. We hung a huge blowup of the photograph in the hall, and to this day the kids still stop and search for their image. They know what letter they were, and what they wore, so they're able to pin it down. It was an all-school production that turned out to be memorable. The following year, I printed 400 postcards of one of the other angles taken that day and used it to invite the ninth graders to freshman orientation."

Another celebration Coach Ekstrom enjoyed, and students cooperated with without much urging, was a "Multicultural Day" that hit them right in their perpetually famished bellies. The gym was set up as a First Class culinary festival featuring the trademark foods from the ethnic groups that comprise Mundelein's diverse student body—Italian, French, Mexican, Indian, Irish Catholic, African American, Thai, and Filipino, among others.

Along those same lines, Ekstrom gives a thumbs up to a high-wire First Class role-playing experiment that was not without controversy.

"We had a lesson where the students either wore blindfolds, tied their arms behind their backs, or put aside everything to reflect what it was like to be a quadriplegic. Different groups were led into the gym to get a sense of what life was like for those who struggled with handicaps." The soccer coach brushes off subsequent criticism from some students who felt the exercise was insensitive and disrespectful. "I thought it was cool. It made them sensitive to the problems of others. The students like to put the whole First Class program down, but you could see it was changing them in a positive way. They mocked the ideal of being 'first class,' and how everybody began using that as a catchphrase, but even while mocking it, it was an effective means for them to correct each other. You couldn't deny that the program was working. You could see the changes everywhere."

Mundelein Principal John Davis—who retired after the 1999-2000 school year—was certainly pleased that both the parents and teachers were taking notice of what First Class was accomplishing.

"In the beginning, First Class met every Monday between first and second period for 20 minutes," Davis says. "It was a quick-shot lesson that was focused on a particular topic like using better language. The idea to use the word 'marshmallow' instead of swear words came out of those early classes. That's all I heard for weeks— 'marshmallow'—so I could see the program was having an immediate effect. There were a lot of different social issues they covered as the year progressed. There was a poster contest, with the 94 First Class groups creating their own posters to support the program. Not a single one was defaced. We also had a contest for the logo, creed, and motto. It all went well.

"There was not a lot of resistance. The kids were more passive in their resistance—skipping the class or not participating in the discussion. The teacher resistance was based upon not understanding their roles, duties, and responsibilities. There was concern that it would take time away from their other classes and increase the workload. That didn't really materialize.

"The most immediate results of First Class could be seen in the assemblies. The students were respecting the guest speakers, and behaving during pep rallies. We had them sit with their First Class groups instead of with their friends and classes, and that worked very well in toning things down. The old chants of 'Freshmen Suck!'

went away. They were also asking a lot more questions about what they planned to do, making sure if it was appropriate or not. They would run the assembly programs past me and say 'Does this sound first class?' That was new. They also were using the phrase 'first class' a great deal as buzz words, and it was really having an effect. I'd hear them say 'that's not first class' in the hallways or cafeteria. It started as a joke, but it became serious. In addition, there was a major decrease in the trash on the floor and grounds outside, and in the bad language being used.

"As the classes evolved, we saw a need to make adjustments. Meeting once a week seemed to be too much, while 20 minutes wasn't enough time to get a good discussion going. We decided the second year to have 40-minute classes every other week. Also, in order to reinforce the Student Leaders, we had hour-long sessions with them every Monday from 7 to 8 A.M. before school. The teachers wanted more contact with the Student Leaders to keep things running smoothly, keep it rolling. It forced the students to get up earlier, but they accepted it. We also gave them a half credit for participating, and hired two additional faculty advisors to assist them.

"First Class similarly had a major effect on the way the students were decorating the school at the beginning of the year and during homecoming. That had been a problem area, one we wanted to correct with First Class, and it worked. The students came to me with a plan for the decorations, which I approved. One year they decorated the senior hallway and the route to the gym. It was very classy with posters and balloons and crepe paper.

"During the initial year of First Class, the senior girls came to me and asked to have their pre-homecoming sleepover restored. They promised to behave in a first-class manner, and showed me a plan of their activities. They combined it with a charity fund-raiser, which involved gathering cans of food. They said each girl would bring a 15-dollar deposit to cover any damage. If there wasn't any, they'd get 10 dollars back, and the other 5 dollars would go to the charity. I approved, and it went perfectly. It's been perfect ever since.

"When Columbine happened, we immediately called a staff meeting. It didn't take us long to decide that the place to deal with it was First Class. I was especially glad we had it in place that day because you could feel the fear and tension among the students. They were very emotional and afraid. There was a genuine fear of copycats. We dealt with it head on in First Class, asking them to tell us how safe they felt at Mundelein, and what recommendations they had for making the school safer. We got tremendous feedback from them. They talked about having metal detectors, which we felt was too extreme, and discussed the problem of how to identify and help students who may be feeling alienated and disenfranchised. They also talked about how the First Class program incorporates all the kids and makes them part of a family.

"We didn't have any students that extreme, but we had our kids who wore the trench coats—(The Goths). They had their own issues, but not like the boys at Columbine. They told us they couldn't relate to what happened there, and they were offended that others were comparing them. 'We're not like that,' they said. We asked them to tone down their clothes for a while afterward. 'Right now, that attire is a catalyst to violence,' I explained. They mostly understood. Some had even stopped dressing that way on their own."

Superintendent Tee Newbrough agrees with his principal that First Class not only corrected Mundelein's major problems, but quickly grew into something special. Oddly enough, with Newbrough's track record at Deerfield and Carl Sandburg, where the program started years earlier, the question arises as to why he didn't implement it at Mundelein sooner?

"We were thinking and talking about it in small circles, we just didn't think the program made sense coming from a top-down position. I don't believe in top-down magic where you jam it in. We were looking for more traditional ways to deal with our problems. Then Karen's kids came along and accelerated the process.

"The best example of how it worked with us was the assembly the first day of school the initial year. We took a risk and reloaded the whole event, mainly by sitting the students with their First Class groups. It turned out to be tremendous. The kids were quiet and respectful. They cheered for the school, and were united instead of divided along class lines. It was like 1956 again! It was the way it used to be, the way assemblies were intended to be.

"That assembly set the tone for the First Class program that followed. We were off and running. And we stayed on top of it as it grew. We worked on it and developed it further. We were constantly evaluating the curriculum and the training of the kids, and it got better and better. Both the students and faculty worked hard at it, writing the lessons and interacting with each other. The Student Leaders became more skilled and experienced. The topics improved. We started giving a service credit to the students for attending. The program was systemized and locked in as part of the school day. We hardwired it in so it couldn't go away, or wasn't dependant upon one innovator like Karen Royer, or a principal or superintendent.

"I'd often walk around the school and ask people 'How's First Class going?' In a large part, the answers were positive. Over time, there was an increased level of acceptance. The only negatives would be specific to that day. They'd say, 'It wasn't that great of a discussion today. We didn't have a broad base of participation. That topic didn't work so well.' They usually gave me real honest answers.

"What's really telling is the number of students who volunteer to be Student Leaders. That's one of the things that pleases me the most. We've been at well over a hundred each year with no sign of losing momentum. You really can't understand the impact of something like this until you have a kid come up to you and say, 'I want to be a First Class Student Leader next year.'"

Newbrough was also pleased to report that the 2000-2001 year opened with minimal toilet paper streaming in the wind. "It was just a few strands here and there," he says with a laugh. "One tree. We nabbed the culprits and they had to do extra collation work for the principal. You always have that 1 percent who want to enter the new era in a manner that is not socially acceptable. The First Class strategy didn't work with these two, so we relied upon another— coppers."

To reward the rest of the student body, Mundelein's new principal, Hillyn Sennholtz, thanked the students for tastefully decorating the school by allowing them to place their handprints in red paint on a specified section of a white wall near the main entry staircase. Nearly 200 participated. The risk here is that the new 'privilege' is dangerously reminiscent of some old vandalism. It was a similar rash of handprints back in 1995 that helped shut down the Senior Girls Sleepover. "This time, it wasn't all over the place without permission," Newbrough points out, giving his support to the more controlled display.

The Superintendent also noted, with a measure of glee, that the students have yet to locate Sennholtz's distant house. That means the first-week tradition of T-papering the principal's home, and depositing toilets and broken furniture on his or her yard among other things, has finally been interrupted as well. That prank had been carried on, without fail, at John Davis house for more than a decade. "It was fun-loving, but I'm hoping that has been retired with Davis," Newbrough says, keeping his fingers crossed.

Most folks in the Mundelein community feel that the best way to honor Davis, the respected long-time principal, is to make sure the First Class program he helped start is never retired. "It's a successful program that has been reinforced in our school," Newbrough agrees. "First Class is the cornerstone for building everything else. It's proved to be an excellent forum for talking about school safety. The small group structure has encouraged students to talk and become involved. It forges a connection between students and teachers, and reduces the chance of a student feeling isolated, disenfranchised and disengaged, and doing something tragic."

And just in case a disengaged kid falls through the cracks, the Superintendent has a plan to cover that as well. "We have a system where we take students' pictures at random during the day and display them on the monitors to get their attention. Kids love to see photos of themselves and often crowd around the monitors. In between is the message 'It's okay to tell' with a phone number that they can use to report any disturbing behavior or vandalism they may have witnessed. We want them to know if they see another student, say, carrying a weapon, that 'it's okay to tell,' even if they do it anonymously.

Newbrough takes special pride in pointing out that thanks to recent innovations, he can now say that he's not asking his students to do anything he's not doing. Since 1998, Mundelein has had an adult First Class program among the faculty and administrators. "I take my seat along with the rest of them. We meet about once a month in groups of 10 or so. The most recent time, before the new year started, we were asked to identify the three greatest strengths of the school, and one area that needs to be improved."

The improvement the Super's group came up with concerned the sometimes disjointed lines of communication from teachers to division heads to the principal to the superintendent, and the need to keep things like student punishments consistent from day to day. They also discussed the proper dress code for teachers on the first day of school and on parents' night. At another Adult First Class meeting they discussed the pending dilemma of reaching student capacity. In 2000–2001, Mundelein approached its 2,100-student limit with a record enrollment of 1,946. "That's getting close," Newbrough said. "There were a lot of good proposals and suggestions that came out of it."

Newbrough points out that Adult First Class, boiled to its essence, accomplishes the same things as the student program—a chance to expand one's circle of friends, a feeling of belonging, and a curb against isolation. "The success of the student First Class program contributed to the creation of its adult counterpart. It was a natural next step. Like the students, we plan to deal with more topics and issues like racism, cultural diversity, sexuality, lifestyles, gender, social status, age discrimination, and things like that. It should prove to be interesting."

While looking forward to those debates, Newbrough promises not to lose touch with the student program that has changed his school so dramatically. "There's a bunch of kids who hang out near my door. Now, when I tell them to watch their language or take off a hat, they roll their eyes less and less. First Class is here at Mundelein to stay!"

PART 2

REFINING "FIRST CLASS" AND TAKING THE SHOW ON THE ROAD

CHAPTER 8

SMOKING OUT THE BUGS

As with any start-up program, those doing the trailblazing are also the ones who experience all the bumps and bruises. Overall, the First Class concept has been a resounding success wherever it's been instituted. However, that's not the same as saying there weren't mistakes made along the way.

The trouble is, trying to ferret out the diamonds from the coal can be a tricky process. The views and opinions of the participants, especially those offered by the students, are highly subjective and often conflict from person to person. What one First Class leader saw as the program's weakness, another cites as one of its strengths. A topic that went over big in one class, laid an egg in another. A role-playing game that engaged the students in room 305, bored the gang in room 306.

Taking this into consideration, it's still worthwhile to consider the warnings and advice of the students, teachers, and administrators who lived through the First Class experience—if only to toss it all into a bubbling cauldron, and see if it produces a stew that another start-up school might find palatable.

Original Mundelein founder Billy Zasadil, '98, previously noted that he had trouble with his initial class because of a teacher who wouldn't sit back and allow him to lead. He mentions that as being one of the major hurdles any new First Class program must overcome. "The teachers have got to learn to back off and let the students run this. It's the only way it will work, and the only way the other students will listen and respect it. If the teachers can't do this, there will be continued problems."

In addition, Zasadil feels that the weekly classes were overdoing it. "I think it was too frequent. Once a week was too much. We ran out of material by the end of the year. We were beating a dead horse. Maybe it would work better to have it every other week."

The alternate-week concept was indeed tried the second year at Mundelein. It was eventually scraped because students and teachers felt that wasn't enough, and that the classes lost momentum during the "dark" weeks.

Shane Chareonchump, a second-year M-Team member, agrees with Zasadil that meddling teachers who couldn't give up the reigns were a major problem, one that he suffered through his first year as well. This phenomena was especially prevalent when the Student Leader was weak or unskilled. Such a scenario complicates things further because a teacher's natural instinct is to jump in to keep the class from sinking. However, both Zasadil and Chareonchump prefer that the teachers show restraint and allow the classes to sink or swim with their Student Leader.

Chareonchump also had a problem with the timing of the summer training sessions. "Our year, they had it the two days before school started. I think that was bad because it was like having school start two days early for us. I think it would have been better to have it in the middle of the summer."

There was also a problem, according to Chareonchump, with topics going on too long. "We talked about sexual harassment for two months. That got really old. We were getting sick of it."

Branden Happ, '99, didn't like the policy that was instituted in later years that enabled underclassmen to be class leaders. "When I was a senior, my leader was a sophomore, maybe a junior, so I didn't listen to her. I didn't cooperate."

Original freshman founder, spunky Jennifer Bouteille, is naturally full of suggestions. "The classes were moved to Mondays one year and I don't think that worked. The students are too burned out on Mondays. You had to pull their legs to get them to talk. That year, I kept saying, 'Okay, I know it's Monday, but let's get going.' I would have kept it on Wednesday. That's right in the middle of the week when things are happening all around. We've already had two days of experiences to talk about. Plus, we could get our lesson plans on Monday and have two days to prepare, rather than trying to prepare over the weekend, or getting the plans Monday morning.

"My senior year, they changed the classes to every other week. I didn't like that. We lost momentum. I think it's important to have the classes every week; otherwise, the students can't remember the subjects.

"One of the worst things were the Student Leaders who would simply read the topic sheets to the class. That was terrible. Can you imagine a student reading, 'Get in a group of five. Now everybody, talk to the person on your right?' People would look at them and say, 'What are you talking about?' The Student Leaders really needed to be prepared. If I saw someone do that, I'd take them aside and say, 'Next time, read it before you get to class!'

"Sexuality topics didn't go anywhere. No one in high school wants to talk about being a gay or lesbian, so we got nothing out of that. Racism and diversity, those subjects worked better, at least at Mundelein. I don't think we ever even touched upon religion. We really didn't know how to bring it up. It's not an interesting topic for students. The best thing to do is simply find out what the students want to talk about. The Student Leaders need to know what the hot topics are at your school. You can try religion, but if no one cares, go somewhere else. Decision-making scenarios usually go over well, such as the basic honesty issue. Say, for example, if you find a wallet, would you take it? Would you take the money and give back the credit cards? These types of things worked well. Role playing, ice breakers, name games—these are easy ways to get everyone involved, but they don't always succeed. The ice-breaker games worked with the Student Leaders during training, but didn't go as well in the actual classes where the people are less involved."

Graham Beatty, 2001, was disappointed that the program didn't remain stable and streamlined. Karen Royer, the French teacher who helped ignite the First Class movement at Mundelein, retired in 1999, and this appears to have had an impact. "There were different people running it in different years, and it didn't seem to have the same plans or structure. I think that hurt it in the long run. It wandered away from the original goals of school spirit, pride, and respect.

"We also had a role-playing game where we tied our legs together, or tied an arm behind our back. The point was to give us a sense of what it was like for someone who is disabled. It didn't work right and it turned out being disrespectful. Another problem was that many of the topics were too obvious. There wasn't much to talk about and elaborate on. They were open-and-shut subjects, like hard drugs— too clear as to what was good or bad, so there was no real learning process and no teaching going on when that happened.'

TJ Waskey, 2000, said his beef was that First Class "wasn't geared toward the good students. I never really had any of the problems we were discussing. I was an Eagle Scout and Boy Scout, and always at the top of my class, so I was getting that stuff (character education) stronger from other places. But I was happy that it cleaned up the school. I would attribute that to First Class."

Luke Hajzl, '98, was expecting the students to have more input into the lesson plans and curriculum. "I was upset that we didn't have control of the topics. It was structured to where we would prepare from a set lesson plan that the teachers had devised. Actually, it wasn't the topics that were the real problem, it was the presentations. We were reading scenarios and short stories to set up the discussions, and the students would laugh and not take it seriously. For example, we would read a prepared story about a guy and girl, 'Johnny' and 'Sally,' going at it in the back seat of a car and the girl ending up pregnant. Then we were supposed to talk about it. The stories would usually sound silly and kill the effect. I'd have rather drawn from our own experiences by telling real stories about things we had gone through, or people we knew. I myself have seen people get hurt, seen them cry, over these sex issues. Girls are forced into sex before they're ready by peer pressure and feel terrible about it afterward. That could have been a solid discussion, but not when it was about Johnny and Sally in the back seat. It was the same for drugs and alcohol. We should have drawn from our own experiences. First Class wasn't supposed to be a lecture. It was supposed to be a group discussion to get everybody involved, and reading those teacher-prepared texts made it more of a lecture. It was harder for the students to be open and honest about themselves based upon those fictional scenarios. They should let the students write more of the curriculum to make it more real.

"Another problem was the black-and-white structure of the topics as they were handed down. Alcohol was a prime example. The plan pushed abstinence for those underage, and the Student Leader had to follow. Then if the leader was partying at a beer blast later that week, it made him appear hypocritical. I would have set the lesson more toward drinking responsibly, and then giving personal examples of what happened to friends and family who didn't. Or even better, I would have liked the students in my class to tell their own stories about problems they had related to drinking. We needed to interact with each other, not follow a lesson from an authority figure."

As Hajzl's fellow students already alluded, some hot-button social topics one might think would be a hit with today's "anything goes" teenagers actually laid an egg.

"Our discussion about gays flopped. We're a middle class, conservative area, so that's not something high school kids like to deal with. I only knew of two openly gay students during my whole time at Mundelein, and I don't know how active, if at all, they were in their First Class. So usually, instead of talking honestly about it, the students would make jokes or ignore it.'

Karen Royer, although retired, still feels connected to the First Class movement she shepherded from a hallway conversation to a curriculum reality. She therefore has her own suggestions regarding what can be improved, and what bugs to avoid. She starts off by throwing her hat into the ring favoring the weekly classes rather than bi-weekly, monthly, or quarterly.

"I think it's important that the school stops every Monday between 10 and 10:30 A.M. to discuss these issues. And I'd like to see us take on everything, from morality, right and wrong, religion, whatever comes up. Nothing should be avoided. It's that family-dinner aspect again. Unless you address what the kids want, they'll tune out and turn off. I'd also like to see us involve the parents more."

First Class encountered its biggest controversy, Royer says, in December 1999 when they kicked off a semester with a series of stereotyping exercises that were designed to teach the students about subconscious racism. The kids wore name tags identifying themselves as a member of a certain ethnic, religious, or racial group—Irish male, Jewish female, Black male, Mexican, Catholic, Arab, etc.—and the class was supposed to list common negative stereotypes associated with those labels. Another variation had the tag-wearing students listing the 'qualities' themselves and the class was supposed to guess their race or ethnic background. The stereotypes, essentially damning slurs like lazy, tightwad, cheap, bossy, drunken, mean-tempered, brawler, intolerant, fanatical, etc., proved to be dicey.

"When the faculty organizers proposed the lesson plan to the First Class teachers, many of them were appalled," Royer recalls. "Their reaction was 'No way are we going to do this.' So we took it before the joint Student Leader and faculty advisory to work it out. We had 100 students and 100 teachers. We argued for nearly three hours. It was an amazing exchange. The faculty wanted to sugarcoat it, make it strawberries and cream. The kids were saying, 'Let's face reality. What are you trying to protect us from? We've heard these stereotypes all our lives.' In the end, we decided to let the strong classes try it. Those who felt it wouldn't work in their classes could handle it a different way. We fielded 30 to 40 suggestions as to how to approach it differently, a lot of good ideas One of the suggestions was to write the stereotypes on a worksheet rather than call them out in class. The students and faculty eventually came up with an alternate lesson plan that made the same point, but wasn't as 'brutal,' as one teacher described it. The faculty advisory and Student Leaders were then allowed to choose the way they wanted to present it based upon what they knew about their own class.

"It ended up being about half and half. The reports I received described the 'brutal' in-your-face method as very effective. It did what it was supposed to do in making the students realize in an unforgettable fashion how deep-seated those stereotypes are, and how they hurt. Those who chose the milder route ended up having their students ask why they weren't allowed to do the 'hotter' version of the exercise. So the lesson there is that it's best to wade right in, to listen to what the students are saying. If they say they can handle a subject or exercise, we teachers have to let them. It has to be something that's meaningful to them. On the other hand, we also have to be flexible enough to modify it when it calls for that."

Jennifer Bouteille says she rolled the dice and went for the "hotter" version—and came up snake eyes. "People didn't feel comfortable playing that stereotype game. It really fizzled in our class because the impression was that you were speaking about your own feelings, or somebody would think you were speaking about your own feelings. If you said Hispanics were lazy, even under the guidelines of the game, that was too rough. I think with a little alteration you could accomplish the same thing. If you premised the question by saying, 'What stereotypes have you heard said about certain groups,' rather than 'What stereotypes can you name,' that softens it. When I put it that way in my class, it opened things up. They began to talk and list things."

Royer says Bouteille's decision to give it a shot, then rely on some quick thinking to keep it from floundering, was an excellent way to handle the controversy. "In the early years, there's a tendency to avoid the really hot topics. The lessons were carefully designed to be a springboard for discussion, to bring out a topic, but there were topics we avoided. You have to know your community, but you also have to be responsive to the students. I don't recall abortion ever being presented. There are two sides to that and both are intense. I'd be interested in seeing how that would go in a First Class discussion.

"I think overall, the success of First Class depends on tailoring it to your specific school district. My children's school in another district was all white, so the racism issues that were so big at Mundelein wouldn't have been the same there. On the other hand, they had more divisions between those from wealthy families and those who were poor, so that would be the topic they needed to explore. You have to understand your community's needs. And there has to be a bond of trust built up among the students in the class before they'll talk. You can't start off with a hot topic in a new group because they're not ready to open up with each other. High school kids are mostly guarded about their feelings. And the cocky ones who speak out tend to be the least self-confident."

The respected French teacher also cautions that First Class is a long-term process that shouldn't be judged too quickly. "You need four years to fully evaluate it. In the first year there's going to be some dramatic changes, but there will also be resistance. The second year will be a sense of 'Okay, it's here to stay.' The third year is 'Okay, what will we talk about now?' And with the fourth year comes a sense of acceptance of how the whole idea is benefiting the student as a person.

"You also have to keep pounding away at the freshmen. That's critical every year because they often come into high school with the thought that they are free from childhood rules. And every year this new group of kids arrives with a fresh need to share their thoughts and feelings, especially on topics that were discussed in the past among the upperclassmen."

In other words, sometimes you have to give the new jockeys a chance to beat the same ol' dead horse.

Royer lists these other bumps to avoid when starting up a Character Education program:

- When training Student Leaders, it's important to pull kids from all groups. You need to have the ethnic groups represented, minorities, even the burn-outs. These students tend to step back and not participate, especially when it comes to volunteering as leaders, so there needs to be an extra effort made in approaching and recruiting these kids.

- The person selected to be the Faculty Coordinator should be aware that it's a big job. It was bigger than I ever imagined. We had to come up with a new lesson every week for 1,600 kids. There were 100-plus leaders to train and stay in constant communication with. The administration needs to give the First Class coordinator the time needed to do the job.

- First Class must be kept on the front burner at all times. It needs to be fresh and alive.

- You have to get everybody to buy into it. In schools where character education is instituted from the top-down, there's going to be a problem getting the kids to go for it. When it comes bottom-up from the kids, it takes extra effort to get the faculty to support it.

- Funding can be a problem. You should have access to money. There are times when you need to treat the students with pizza, M&Ms®, or other rewards, so if you have to, pound the pavement to get the community to donate.

- Scheduling is important. Where do you put it in the school day? This is where you need the administrative support. The unions can be a problem here. You can't tread on their toes. Our union wanted stipends for the teachers. I found that hard to swallow because the return on investment of students learning respect was going to benefit the teachers.

- The teachers must start off excited about the program and remain excited. If they're not, you'll be spending extra time and energy trying to overcome that.

- The teachers have to turn their classes over to the Student Leaders. They have to loosen their grip. The students must always feel that they own the program. This was very difficult for some of the faculty to do. Many could never arrive at doing it.

- On the other hand, the teachers can't back totally off and leave the room either. They need to be there at all times acting as facilitators.

- There should be a reward system for good behavior. Everybody likes to win and accomplish things. If students have lost privileges in the past because of bad behavior, they should be returned through their First Class program.

"In summary, you have to keep working with the kids," says Royer. "If you do, you'll see the benefits. And remember, it won't fix everything. There will still be problems. But it will fix a lot of things."

Dean of Students John Ahlgrim, the football coach who spends a big part of his day interacting "up close and personal" with the students, not surprisingly mirrored some of the same concerns. "It's far more effective if you can get the kids to be reflective about things from their own lives instead of providing them with a fabricated story. Kids like to talk about real experiences rather than specified lesson-plan scenarios. They need to build up enthusiasm regarding things they know about. When we realized that, we spent less time trying to create fictional lessons and more time looking for experiences that the students know about.

"Another hurdle we faced was the unreal demands placed upon the Student Leaders. Over the years, we learned to have a realistic view of what that role was like. We (teachers and administrators) thought it would be easier than it was. At that age, kids aren't always sure who they are and what they want to be yet, and here we were putting them in front of the class in peer leadership roles. It's a great challenge for us to prepare them for that. We've gotten better because both the teachers and students understand it better now."

Ahlgrim also favors a looser structure that allows the students to respond to current events. "They should use the moment to reflect upon their lives. For example, when Columbine hit you could see the devastation and impact on everybody, especially those of us in a high school environment. We were able to respond to that immediately in our First Class groups, and that helped. I'd like to see us react to more things in that way, to take negative experiences and make something positive out of it. There needs to be a balance between the prepared lessons and the ability to be responsive to events that happen around us. That's not easy. Often, I'd ask a First Class advisor, 'How did it go?' They'd say, 'It went great, but we didn't do what was on the paper.' That's fine. If the lesson takes them in another direction that is legitimate and manageable, we want to encourage that. But again, it goes back to an effective Student Leader who has the ability to shift focus when it's warranted.

"Another mistake we made involved the role-playing exercises we scheduled early on. When some of them didn't work, we assumed the students were bored or lethargic. That wasn't true. They just weren't ready. They needed to build a trust before they got into the skits and role playing. Some of the things we asked them to do that first year were, in all honesty, ridiculous. High school kids don't need that kind of thing. They need the right message and the way to express themselves."

Soccer coach Dave Ekstrom, who helped develop the initial First Class curriculum, emphasized the same problem. "We created a very ambitious lesson plan that included a lot of role-playing exercises, touchy-feely stuff. Some of the teachers and students were uncomfortable with those more intimate activities because they didn't know each other. They were lumped together in the 4-4-4-4 class groupings, so they were basically all new to each other and hadn't formed a comfort level. We got away from that in later years in favor of videos and discussions, and pushed those participation things farther into the semester after the students and teachers had grown more comfortable with each other. We learned that we had to do team-building exercises before we could go into the role-playing skits. That first year, we tried to jump right to that step, and it wasn't real successful."

Ekstrom adds that the slow start hampered the program in subsequent years as well, causing the students and administrators to rethink the once innovative and highly praised 4-4-4-4 structure and experiment with single-class groupings. "That might help get things started a little quicker," he says. "The hardest thing is finding lessons that the kids are interested in. A good lesson that hits home with them will get any class involved. Give them a topic that misses, and even the best class can't wait to get out of there. That's why giving students input in developing the curriculum is so important."

Mundelein Superintendent Tee Newbrough remains so pumped by First Class he had to struggle to come up with any bugs. "I think if anything, we should have been a little better getting full support from the teachers that initial year. When the kids were doing their thing and were all excited, some teachers were less passionate and supportive than they could have been. They didn't help the Students Leaders who hit dead air in class, or someone dominating the discussions. We probably should have had more in-service training of the staff prior to launching the program."

Like Ekstrom, he also mentions the class groupings as something they've had to wrestle with over the years. "I know that the 4-4-4-4 diversity has been one of the program's strengths, but we feel that different topics might work better with different age groups. Date rape and sexual harassment might be more appropriate for seniors than freshmen."

Newbrough is keenly aware of what effect the 'age alike' First Class groups might have on the tinderbox assemblies. Will it signal a return to chanting class rivalries? "They'll still be sitting with their First Class groups, and those groups will be scattered among the different classes, so we won't have all the seniors sitting together screaming at the freshmen like before. There's been a lot of thought and evaluation that went into this change. It will be interesting to see how it turns out."

At Deerfield High, where First Class was spawned more than a decade ago, the founders have had the opportunity to see how a lot of things have turned out. Deerfield's First Class structure and curriculum has gone through enough mutations to make a hot-headed X-Man like Wolverine proud. New principal and Deerfield veteran Scott Kasik reports that they've spent a lot of time ironing out the bugs and making adaptations over the past decade.

"We didn't want First Class, from any perspective, to feel like just another set of rules. We never wanted it to come across as adults wanting kids to behave the way the adults wanted them to. Too often in the early days I'd hear a teacher admonish a kid, 'That's not first class' in a punishing tone. That had a negative effect and defeated what we were trying to accomplish. We wanted them to say 'That's first class!' when the kids did something right. We couldn't let First Class evolve into just another period where adults were telling the kids how we wanted them to behave. We always had to temper back on that, and not give into the temptation to use it that way. The teachers needed to be aware that it was a student-oriented program, and that was its value. It's there for the students.

"First Class is a high-maintenance program. The teachers and administrators have to keep their fingers on the pulse of what's happening with it at all times. The message has to be kept fresh, and you've got to maintain the high expectations of the program after the initial years when all the most dramatic results are seen. You can't let a sense of complacency set in, the 'What's the big deal? Things are going fine. We don't need this anymore.' You can't take it for granted, especially with new staff members. They don't know how bad it was before First Class, so it can be hard for them to understand the need. No matter how well things are at school, you still have to find new and creative ways to keep it going.

"I remember meeting with students one year when our basketball team was really good, and discussing how they were not to respond to the negative chants and goading from the students at the opposing schools. 'You really expect a lot from us," one student commented. 'Yes, we do!' I responded. I explained that in the early years, First Class was more 'What we do.' After the program had been in effect a few years, First Class became 'What we are.' It's important to know the difference, and to integrate it into the entire school.

"Along those lines, you can't focus on the star jocks and head cheerleaders or even the First Class leaders. You have to focus on those students who don't get formal recognition. We alerted our teachers to watch out for things these 'average' students did right and to acknowledge them. We sometimes send 30 to 40 letters home a month to the students' parents telling them about something good their child did, and we highlight it in a school bulletin. One time a teacher noticed that a freshman girl, a Special Needs student, was off by herself at one of our dances. A popular senior girl went over and talked with her for a long time. We noted that in our bulletin in a way that praised the senior but didn't embarrass the freshman. Another student found a 100-dollar bill in the hallway and brought it to me. I thought that was extraordinary. No one ever claimed it, and the student never asked for it even then. That person was publicly recognized in the bulletin. One teacher recognized her entire class. She took a photo and sent it home to all their parents along with a letter praising the whole group. This is how we incorporated all the students into the rewards system."

Taking everyone's perceived "bugs" into consideration, character education might come across as a lot of intense effort that still produces an abundance of rough sledding. With all the glitches, booby traps, potholes and conflicting opinions, is this First Class thing really worth the trouble? Is it actually catching on outside a small, interwoven area of Illinois? You'll probably be shocked by the answer.

CHAPTER 9

THE SPREAD

My administration will give taxpayers new incentives to donate to charity, encourage after-school programs that build character, and support mentoring groups that shape and save young lives. We must give our children a spirit of moral courage, because their character is our destiny. We must tell them, with clarity and confidence, that drugs and alcohol can destroy you, and bigotry disfigures the heart. Our schools must support the ideals of parents elevating character and abstinence from afterthoughts to urgent goals. We must help protect our children, in our schools and streets, by finally and strictly enforcing our nation's gun laws. Most of all, we must teach our children the values that defeat violence.
—President George W. Bush

Mike Koehler, Ph.D, the author of 15 educational workbooks and a member of the original First Class teacher focus group at Deerfield

High, says he knew they were on to something big back in the early 1990s. "This thing is going to fly all over the country. Character Education is going to go wild."

Looking back, that might be viewed as an understatement. The smoldering fire flamed in early 1996 when the *Chicago Tribune* got wind of what was happening at Deerfield and sent a reporter to check it out. The resulting half-page spread in the Sunday paper made Koehler look like a seer.

"After the story ran, more than 150 schools from around the nation contacted us," Deerfield Principal and First Class creator John Scornavacco remembers. "It was amazing. There were so many schools dealing with instability and lack of respect. They asked if they could send task forces to learn more about what we were doing."

Scornavacco admits that he and his fellow administrators and teachers became almost giddy with the success and attention. "We put on a dog and pony show for them. The students, parents, faculty members, administrators, and even the school board members were involved. It started to become a real distraction, so we had to change things. Instead of just putting on the show whenever somebody came to town, we specified three dates during the school year when we would host other schools and hand out our materials. I stressed that these were only guidelines that should be adapted to each individual school, but I've seen other places use our program word for word. All they did was cross out 'Deerfield' and pencil in the name of their own institution."

After a while, even those set times became too much of an intrusion. Scornavacco says he now usually goes on the road to make presentations, or hands the invitation off to current Deerfield Principal Scott Kasik, or former Deerfield Special Education teacher Bob Gottlieb, currently the principal of nearby North Shore Academy. Kasik offers additional insight into why the "dog and pony show" was retired.

"The overwhelming reaction from around the nation caught us by surprise. We weren't sure how to handle it. When the other schools started calling and visiting us, our students felt neglected for a while, or felt they were being used as guinea pigs on display. The program was getting a lot of attention, and our students believed that the success was getting to our heads and we weren't focusing on them any-more. The sentiment was, 'Are you doing this for us, or for someone else?' We had to be very careful about that, eventually scaling back and altering some of the procedures for dealing with the visits from other schools so our students wouldn't feel this way. By staying close to our students, and keeping our fingers on the pulse of First Class, we were able to quickly determine how they felt and react to it. First Class must be monitored all the time, even when it's successful."

Despite the bruised feelings of his students, Scornavacco stead-fastly believes that First Class is far too important to keep to themselves. "It will work well in any school, even intercity institu-tions. We've seen it set up in tough places and gain the same positive results. It's been used in middle and elementary schools as well."

Actually, since Deerfield started their program, and Mundelein infused it with new energy with the bottom-up, grassroots approach, it's been spreading like wildfire. In 1995, the United States Depart-ment of Education jumped on board in a huge way, offering grant money to states interested in hopping on the Character Education bandwagon. As of the "Space Odyssey" year of 2001, 46 states have applied for the grants, and 37 have been awarded, receiving a total of $25 million. (Addendum 2 on page 165 lists the recent awards.) Most of the remaining states have their applications pending. Puerto Rico, a U.S. Commonwealth, and The Virgin Islands, a U.S. Terri-tory, have sent in applications as well.

It should be noted, however, that virtually all these grants have been used to institute Character Education test projects in a handful of schools in these states, meaning that the vast majority of American public schools are without instruction of this nature.

Former U.S. Secretary of Education Richard W. Riley is nonethe-less proud of the officially named "Partnerships in Character Education Pilot Projects Program" that was instituted during his recent reign under the Clinton administration as the nation's top edu-cator. "Good citizenship, compassion and respect for others are qualities just as important to learning as high standards in math, sci-ence, and reading. . . . School is where most young people spend most of their time outside the home. With these grants, schools and com-munities can reinforce parents in helping students learn to make good choices and be positive members of society throughout their lives."

The goals of this federal "partnership" are listed as:

- Reducing discipline problems
- Improving student grades
- Increasing participation in extracurricular activities
- Strengthening parent and community involvement

The pioneer states have also been asked to establish a clearinghouse, usually through an easily accessible Internet web site, for the distribution of materials and information about character education.

A similar resource web site, one that is not part of a state grant experiment, is the "Character Counts!" curriculum offered by the Josephson Institute of Ethics (*http://www.charactercounts.org*). This program had been adopted by many states and nonprofit organizations. In addition, the Deerfield/Mundelein method will soon be available in an accompanying workbook, *First Class Character Education Activities Program* (© 2001, Prentice Hall) authored by pioneers Mike Koehler and Karen Royer.

Even before the Feds got involved, some cities and states were organizing and funding their own character education programs. St. Louis constructed a thriving effort called the Personal Responsibility Education Process (PREP), which is operated and funded by an educational consortium known as the Cooperating School Districts. In less than a decade, PREP has reached more than 390 schools, 13,000 teachers, and 213,000 students. Nearly 50 businesses, foundations, and individuals serve as community partners. According to PREP coordinator Linda McKary, their goal "is to weave character education throughout the school day, integrating it into the school mission, curriculum, discipline policies, after-school activities and reform initiatives."

In Georgia, state representative Carl Von Epps introduced House Bill 363 in 1999 to provide for the creation and development of a character education curriculum in his state's public schools. The bill passed the Georgia House 165-0, the Senate 50-0, and was signed into law. A year later, it was amended to require that local schools implement the program at all grade levels.

Some states like Arizona have taken their case to the public, putting a character education initiative on the ballot. Arizona's mission statement reads:

"Arizona will be recognized and respected nationally as a model state by providing voluntary education and training on the core values of trustworthiness, respect, responsibility, fairness, caring and citizenship to educators, leaders of youth nonprofit organizations and children in Arizona. This will be made possible through collaborations with businesses; educators; community organizations; the State of Arizona; state and local agencies that deal with parents and youth; Sovereign Nations; all other levels of government; youth sports programs; and all stakeholders that work with youth."

The language created for the successful November 2000 Arizona ballot drive, confusing as it might be, gives further insight into how the concepts behind the movement that started in Illinois is spreading.

15-154.01. FEDERAL CHARACTER EDUCATION MATCHING GRANT PROGRAM

A. Any public or charter school that teaches a character education curriculum pursuant to section 15-719 is eligible for a state-matching grant of up to one thousand five hundred dollars annually. The school shall provide matching monies from any lawful source.

B. The character education program shall be an age-specific, stand-alone character education curriculum with the following elements:

1. Applicable definitions for character qualities that include at least five of the following attributes:

(a) attentiveness.

(b) caring.

(c) citizenship.

(d) compassion.

(e) diligence.

(f) discernment.

(g) forgiveness.

(h) generosity.

(i) gratefulness.

(j) initiative.

(k) orderliness.

(l) respect.

(m) responsibility.

(n) sincerity.

(o) trustworthiness.

(p) virtue.

(q) wisdom.

(For the complete description of the initiative, see Addendum 2 on page 165.)

Arizona Governor Jane Hull, a fervent character education backer, additionally offers these suggestions for developing a statewide program:

- Offer the training on a voluntary basis at no charge to those being trained—if they agree to implement it into their curriculum.

- Give specific expectations to those requesting the training. This includes participating in pre and post program research.

- Use a character education program that is nonpartisan and not religious based.

- Involve the community, business leaders, and other collaborating partners.

- To ensure the long-term sustainability of the training, either found a nonprofit organization to eventually carry on the training opportunity, or work with another nongovernmental entity that will help support the initiative for years to come.

- Remember, research has shown that an effective character education training program that is incorporated in the curriculum *can* reduce alcohol and drug use, reduce suspensions, reduce absenteeism, reduce youth crime, and improve the level of respect and morale in an organization.

"Today's children are tomorrow's leaders in Arizona," Hull adds. "I believe if we come together as parents, teachers, youth leaders— and communities support and teach the values of trustworthiness, respect, responsibility, fairness, caring, and citizenship—our children will be happier, more productive, and better citizens."

Meanwhile, Arizona Republican State Senator David Peterson of Mesa differs with Governor Hull on the voluntary issue. He is working to pass legislation that would make the program mandatory.

Others states, like California, Texas, Maryland, South Dakota, and Colorado, to name a few, went after the federal grants almost from the moment the ink dried on the applications. California officially evaluated its "pilot program" after four years and concluded that:

- School suspensions are down.
- Parents, staff, and students feel their school is a safer place.
- Student attendance is up.
- Staff, parent, and student attitudes about schools improved.
- School community speaks a common character language.
- Character is a visible part of school climate.

(For more specific details on the results of these and other state programs, see Addendum 2 on page 165)

Whether it's mandatory or voluntary, a state ballot issue or a federally funded pilot program, the rapid spread of character education has brought support from all corners—and surprisingly enough, a few detractors as well. First, the supporters. Former McDonnell Douglas Chairman Sanford N. McDonnell has made character education one of his major, post-business-life focuses. He now serves as the Chairman of the Character Education Partnership (CEP – 1-800-988-8081), a nonpartisan coalition of organizations and individuals working to "bring moral character and civic virtue" to children.

"We in the business world don't want young people coming into our employment and into our communities who are brilliant, but dishonest; who have great intellectual knowledge, but don't really care about others; who have highly creative minds, but are irresponsible," McDonnell chides. "All of us in business and the entire adult community need to do our part in helping build young people of high character. There isn't a more critical issue in education today."

Bob Chase, President of the National Education Association, readily accepts that it's the school system's responsibility to avoid creating the "brilliant but dishonest" graduates McDonnell fears. "I believe that a values vacuum exists in American society, and that teachers must not be casual or apologetic about confronting it. We must make an explicit commitment to formal character education. We must integrate character education into the fabric of the curriculum and into extracurricular activities. We must train teachers in character education—both pre-service and in-service. And we must consciously set about creating a moral climate within our schools."

Charles C. Haynes, a columnist and scholar for the *Freedom Forum*, has little patience for those who try to sidestep character education on political grounds. "There are those educators and parents who think that schools should stay out of the values business. They even blame the First Amendment for their inactions, claiming that public schools must be 'neutral about values' in order to avoid promoting or inhibiting religion. But this is a bogus argument. First Amendment neutrality concerning religion in public schools doesn't mean neutrality on values. Schools can and must teach those core moral values widely agreed upon by the community, values such as honesty, responsibility, respect, and caring. True, teachers can't invoke religious authority. But they can find ways to help students of all faiths or none understand, adopt, and practice core moral values. And they can teach about the various ways in which religions address such values. Some see character education as a distraction from the 'real work' of education. But far from being an add-on, character education is essential to carrying out the academic mission of the school."

Haynes, in another article, says teachers need to be instructed from the start that character education is part of their jobs. "Most deans of education schools believe that core moral values should be taught in public schools. But they readily admit that their institutions aren't doing much about it. Why? It may be that some schools of education are still influenced by an earlier era when it was widely believed that schools should be neutral on values. There's still a fear of 'indoctrination,' of any kind of confusion as to whether teaching values means imposing religion. . . . Public schools promote values one way or another all day long. The issue isn't whether or not to teach values. The issue is which values to teach and how to do it. . . . There is no quick fix for the moral breakdown that causes students to shoot students or to take drugs, join gangs, or self-destruct in other ways. But character education—more than metal detectors or police in the hallways—is the most effective, long-term strategy that public schools can adopt."*

Kevin Ryan, President of the Center for the Advancement of Ethics and Character at Boston University, is another strong proponent of

---

*Haynes' columns can be found at *www.freedomforum.org*

teaching values to children. In an article he wrote for *The American Enterprise*, Ryan stated: "The character education of our children is fast becoming the topic du jour. In his 1996 State of the Union address, President Clinton urged American schools to perform character education. . . . Critics like the ACLU see the new character education movement as the stalking horse for the return of Christianity to the schools. Many Christians, on the other hand, are appalled by the idea of the public schools moving into the moral domain, a domain they see as the province of the family and the church. They believe the character education movement signals a new offensive by the secular humanist, who has damaged our schools enough already. . . . But there is one brute fact that all sides should acknowledge: The schools cannot get out of the business of character education. Parents cannot turn over their child to the schools for 13 impressionable years and then prevent the school from having a profound impact on his character. Schools, by their nature, cannot be morally neutral. Indeed, they are moral cauldrons of rewards and punishments, winners and losers, and a continuing parade of issues calling out to be labeled 'right' and 'wrong.'

". . . While character education may have become an educational bandwagon, it is no newcomer to our schools. . . . In 1697, the Massachusetts colonists passed our first school establishment law, called the Old Deluder Act, for the express purpose of teaching children how to read the Bible, so as to resist the snares of that Old Deluder, Satan."

Although few can argue that teaching kids to resist ye Ol' Deluder, and all that concept stands for, can't be bad, count author William Kilpatrick (*Why Johnny Can't Tell Right From Wrong*) among those who feel the character education movement is doomed to once again suffocate under the weight of liberal political restraints. Also writing in *The American Enterprise*, Kilpatrick warns: "What character education is really about—the cultivation of virtues through the formation of good habits—is so far removed from the current educational mind-set as to be almost incomprehensible. In attempts to assimilate the idea, today's educators have been forced to distort and dilute it. . . . Effective character formation . . . seems to require institutions with an allegiance to common cultural ideals. . . . Right now, the public schools appear to be marching in the exact opposite direction—toward the worship of diversity and multiculturalism.

Educators may talk about character education, but they are actually promoting the concept of multiculturalism. And, as it is currently practiced, multiculturalism is the antithesis of a common culture. In essence, it is the revival of the old dogma of cultural relativism: Each culture is so different from every other culture that no culture has the right to make judgments about any other culture. From here, of course, it is only a short step to moral relativism (no individual has the right to make judgments about the behavior of other individuals)—a step that educators are willing to take. Multiculturalism provides a heightened sense of group and ethnic consciousness, which makes it nearly impossible for schools to create a common school culture and common behavioral expectations.

". . . If public schools were once reasonably effective at the job of character formations, it was largely because the school ethos could be tied to the group-transcending visions provided by Western, Judeo-Christian tradition. The historical situation that made this possible has passed. Now it is politically incorrect for schools to have any special allegiance to Western culture or religion. . . . Helping students feel comfortable with whatever they happen to want to do is not conducive to their developing solid virtues. . . . Effective character formation, once within the reach of all public schools, is now possible, for the most part, only in private and parochial schools. . . . Those who hope for a revival of character education in the public schools argue that if it was done before, why not again. But all the evidence suggests that short of some dramatic and probably traumatic historical reversal, that blessed state cannot be recaptured. It's time to face up to that fact. Character education in public schools doesn't have a prayer."

Eighteenth-century physician and statesman Dr. Benjamin Rush, a signer of the Declaration of Independence, offered a similar warning at the dawn of a free America: "I know there is an objection among many people to teaching children doctrines of any kind, because they are liable to be controverted. But let us not be wiser than our Maker. If moral precepts alone could have reformed mankind, the mission of the Son of God into all the world would have been unnecessary."

P. Andrew Sandlin, author and Executive Director of the Chalcedon Foundation, sits squarely among the skeptics as well. Sandlin, quoted in the *Federalist Digest*: "When you abolish Jesus Christ and the Bible from not only the classroom but also a two-minute time slot before high school football games, you are not practicing religious neutrality. You are substituting a new religion for an old one. When classroom instruction is anchored in Darwinian evolution, state socialism, and a passionate amorality, you are looking at a New Established Religion—secular humanism. There is no religious neutrality in this, and there never could be. Secular humanism has supplanted orthodox Christianity as the unofficially established religion of the United States. Government schools are the chief hotbed of this new religion. It is relentlessly anti-Christian."

Creators Syndicate columnist Linda Bowles has protested along related lines. "The belief that government schools are neutral on morality and religion is extraordinarily naive. Once it becomes clear that government schools indoctrinate captive students in the tenets and dogma of humanism to the exclusion of all other religions, it also becomes clear that the government itself is in the business of establishing a state-run, religious monopoly."

Colorado's Commissioner of Education, William J. Moloney, is a rare, high-level public school administrator who is not afraid to speak out on this issue. Moloney's feelings are especially powerful considering what happened at Columbine, a high school under his watch. "Virtually the entirety of our population, whatever their faith, acknowledges God. Through history, our schools like our society have done so as well. This common bond has been a transcendent and unifying element in our nation's life. If by tortured logic, we deny this heritage, we are attacking the sense of unity upon which our civil society depends." (See Addendum 4 on page 193 for more from Moloney.)

Others fear that even as character education spreads, the forces on the opposite end of the political spectrum remain hard at work trying to counter every advance. A Supreme Court decision outlawing prayer before high school athletic contests ignited a storm of controversy in the fall of 2000. Some parents and educators feel the continuing onslaught of such liberal rulings is already beginning to take the wind out of the burgeoning character education movement's sails. Jody McLoud, principal of Roane County High School in Kingston, Tennessee, courageously addressed this roadblock head on in a powerful speech he gave before one of his school's sporting events:

"It has always been the custom at Roane County High School football games to say a prayer and play the National Anthem to honor God and Country. Due to a recent ruling by the Supreme Court, I am told that saying a prayer is a violation of Federal Case Law. As I understand the law at this time, I can use this public facility to approve of sexual perversion and call it an alternate lifestyle, and if someone is offended, that's okay. I can use it to condone sexual promiscuity by dispensing condoms and calling it safe sex. If someone is offended, that's okay. I can even use this public facility to present the merits of killing an unborn baby as a viable means of birth control. If someone is offended, no problem.

"I can designate a school day as earth day and involve students in activities to religiously worship and praise the goddess, mother earth, and call it ecology. I can use literature, videos, and presentations in the classroom that depict people with strong, traditional, Christian convictions as simple-minded and ignorant and call it enlightenment. However, if anyone uses this facility to honor God and ask Him to bless this event with safety and good sportsmanship, Federal Case Law is violated.

"This appears to be at best, inconsistent and at worst, diabolical. Apparently, we are to be tolerant of everything and anyone except God and His commandments. Nevertheless, as a school principal, I frequently ask staff and students to abide by rules with which they do not necessarily agree. For me to do otherwise would be at best, inconsistent and at worst, hypocritical. I suffer from that affliction enough unintentionally. I certainly do not need to add an intentional transgression. For this reason, I shall, 'Render unto Caesar that which is Caesar's,' and refrain from praying at this time. However, if you feel inspired to honor, praise, and thank God, and ask Him in the name of Jesus to bless this event, please feel free to do so. As far as I know, that's not against the law—yet.'"

McLoud, who instituted the Josephson Institute's "Character Counts!" curriculum at his school in 1998, believes that the way such programs are forced to dance around religion, along with the accompanying silence of religious-minded teachers and administrators, is "the crux of the problem," that led to the behavior crisis that has afflicted schools to begin with. "We are in a spiritual battle for our students, and we are not going to find a secular solution. If 'Character Counts' is to live up to its message, the students will eventually discover, 'Gosh, I can't do this without divine intervention.' We can't accomplish our goals with a secular process. If we could, we would have already done it. We are not going to solve these problems without God's help."

While others sympathize with such sentiments, they're not yet ready to toss in the towel. Former Secretary of Education William Bennett, a gung-ho character education supporter and a battle-scarred veteran of high-stakes federal government skirmishes over "political correctness," made character at all costs the theme of an article he wrote for the *Ladies Home Journal* in 1994.

". . . We need to recognize that many of the problems afflicting society today are moral problems, and therefore remarkably resistant to government cures. The real answer to the perils of our time is that we simply must become more civilized. And the best way to become more civilized is to inculcate virtue in our children. Now by 'virtue' I don't mean a kind of moral perfection that none of us is capable of attaining. What I do mean is that we must pay attention to something that every civilized society has given preeminent importance: instilling in our children certain fundamental traits of character—traits like honesty, compassion, courage, perseverance, altruism, and fidelity to one's commitments. . . . We need to agree again on the fundamental purpose of education—which is to provide for the intellectual and moral education of the young. From the ancient Greeks to the founding fathers, moral instruction was considered the central task of education. Until a quarter century or so ago, the consensus was so complete as to go practically unchallenged: Now it's time to go back to basics. Parents should insist on teachers who are willing to discriminate between right and wrong. They should also insist on the school's maintaining policies that reward good behavior and punish bad."

Harold Joe Bishop, Jr., an Army officer turned elementary school teacher, also revisited education history in a paper entitled, "Character Education: Do We Need It?" that he wrote while attending Southwest Texas State University:

"Historically, character development was at the heart of teacher training in America. In order to usher in a new era of popular schooling, nineteenth-century school pioneers, most notably Horace Mann in Massachusetts, sought to create a system of 'Normal Schools' to raise up a new breed of teachers to carry out the new 'common school' mission. No longer was the mission of schooling to be limited to the teaching of the academic basics, rather, it was to serve as an engine of public virtue. The primary impulse for the founding of the Normal School—the precursors to today's school of education—was in fact to prepare teachers of exceptional moral character to shape the moral and intellectual sentiments of young people for life in a republican society. . . . Common sense tells us that values such as compassion, respect, and responsibility build the kind of people we need in society, and enable all of us to better understand and help those who need help before it is too late."

Thomas Jefferson, a strong advocate of separation of church and state in public schools (even before there were public schools), nevertheless saw a need for character-based education: ". . . Their minds are to be informed by education . . . what is right and what is wrong; to be encouraged in habits of virtue and to be deterred from those of vice. . . . These are the inculcations necessary to render the people a sure basis for the structure and order of government."

The International Center for Leadership in Education, based in Rexford, New York (*info@daggett.com*), is another organization that feels strongly enough about character education to develop and offer its own teaching guides. Its mission statement says, in part: "Successful schools—those with the highest levels of student achievement—do not sidestep the issue of character education. They embrace it. In fact, these schools acknowledge that their success is due in large measure to their attention to guiding principals, through which they have been able to create the supportive learning environment that is absolutely essential for students to achieve high standards."

In July 1992—a few months before the rowdy class of 1996 first entered Mundelein High—the previously mentioned Josephson Institute of Ethics brought a group of educators, character education experts, and the heads of various youth organizations to Aspen, Colorado to draft a statement on character education. After three days, they came up with one that still rings true in the new millennium:

". . . The present and future well-being of our society requires an involved, caring citizenry with good moral character. . . . People do not automatically develop good moral character; therefore, conscientious efforts must be made to help young people develop the values and abilities necessary for moral decision making and conduct. . . . Effective character education is based on core ethical values which form the foundation of democratic society, in particular, respect, responsibility, trustworthiness, caring, justice and fairness, and civic virtue and citizenship."

The students gathered outside Karen Royer's French 301 class in 1996 couldn't have said it better.

Circling back to Illinois, the home of Deerfield and Mundelein highs, the University of Illinois Extension now offers character education curriculum development, along with an extensive training program for teachers. As of 2001, more than 5,000 teachers responsible for 93,000 students have taken the classes. The university's mission statement is particularly enthusiastic:

"What does character education look like? How does it feel? Character education looks like young people learning, growing, and becoming. It feels like strength, courage, possibility, and hope. Giving life meaning, purpose, and a future is the collective message educators are sharing with youth in a curriculum that ultimately says, 'Together we can.' Embedded in character education are guidelines for successful living. The language of respect and responsibility navigates the journey to ethical fitness. Students explore education as life and life as learning positive approaches for setting and achieving goals. Students learn that living each day to its fullest means more than waiting for moments here and there. Character education presents life with context, inviting students to listen, share, explore, and reflect. Cultivating knowledge for purposeful living, students learn through literature, art, humanities, and throughout the existing school curriculum the benefits and consequences of behavior. They learn the power of choice. They learn to appreciate the qualities of being human and to share their appreciation at home, in school, and in the community."

And they also learn that although it may seem to be a hoot at the time, it really isn't cool to bathe your homecoming queen in chocolate pudding—especially with newspaper photographers around.

CHAPTER 10

SPECIAL CASES:
THE CIRCLE OF COURAGE
AT SWEAT HOG HIGH

The true test of any character education program is whether it can reach a school's most difficult discipline cases. Many principals segregate these long-term, problematic students in special needs classes that isolate them from the rest of the student body. Although television shows like *Welcome Back Kotter* and *Happy Days* have glamorized these "Sweat Hogs," in reality, they are rarely handsome toughs with hearts of gold pounding beneath their leather jackets— à la Vinnie Barberino and Arthur "The Fonz" Fonzerelli. While we smile at the memory of such lovable characters, portrayed by actors John Travolta and Henry Winkler, the truth is that special needs students are a far less cuddly bunch. They are more likely a defiant group of angry and scarred social misfits ravaged by severe behavioral and emotional problems caused by everything from parental abuse, sexual assaults, anxiety disorders, and learning disorders to genetic mysteries.

In a nutshell, they are not the kind of teenagers who are going to be swept away by perky cheerleaders and gung-ho football captains effusing the wonders of being good. Can a program like First Class even hope to quiet the rage in such young men and women?

If anyone has the answer, it's Bob Gottlieb, Special Ed teacher extraordinaire who just happened to be at Deerfield High when the original First Class program was kicked off in the late 1980s. At the time, Gottlieb was riding herd over a classroom known unaffectionately as "The Cage," a place where Deerfield's real-life Sweat Hogs were kept symbolically "chained up" in their own turbulent world for the entire school day. Designed on the surface as a caring environment tailored to their "special needs," The Cage doubled as a means of keeping its antisocial inhabitants a safe distance away from the fellow students who loathed them, and the teachers who recoiled at the thought of their disruptive ilk careening like time bombs from one class to another. Gottlieb later went on to become principal of North Shore Academy, an alternate school for, if one can imagine, a sub-species of Sweat Hogs who are so unruly they manage to get themselves expelled from places like "The Cage."

"I was in on the initial committee at Deerfield before First Class even had a name," he explains. "At the time, there was a division between the older, veteran teachers and a younger crew that wanted to make changes. We were locked in an 'us and them' situation that was infecting the various departments as well. The superintendent, Jim Warren, brought in a renowned educational consultant named Dick Foster to bring us together. Foster told us he was there to remake the school and the only thing limiting us was our imaginations.

"My interest in being part of this is that I wanted my kids to be integrated, in some part, back into the regular school day. I didn't want them to be viewed as pariahs. With the right encouragement, they could be mainstreamed into such classes as physical education, art, and computer labs. Often, my kids actually showed talent in these areas, and I needed the teachers to help them nurture their natural abilities instead of being afraid of them. At the same time, I wanted to create a school environment that was kinder, and more tolerant, to have the whole faculty work with troubled kids rather than a few isolated teachers and counselors.

"We had a good group of eight to ten teachers and we communicated well. It was the antecedent of the original First Class teachers committee that would form a few months later."

The second incarnation of this faculty group, the one that Gottlieb mentioned was destined to develop First Class, added a few more members, and expanded the scope to include the problems of the entire school, good students and bad. The problems, as previously mentioned, involved a general preponderance of antisocial behavior, vandalism, outrageous pranks, bad language, lack of respect for teachers, litter, graffiti, and the like.

"There were some areas of the school that were like a gauntlet," Gottlieb recalls. "The teachers wouldn't even walk through those hallways. That was not a good climate. That's not the way a school should be. There was also an attitude among the teachers that they weren't trained to intervene with the most difficult kids, especially the ones who weren't 'theirs.' Everybody was in their own world.

"We decided that we, as a faculty, would have to accomplish the corrections that we wanted to make. The old guard and new needed to unite and take ownership of the school to create a positive climate. We also decided that we wouldn't just make a recommendation and pass the buck up to the administration. We were going to do it ourselves. And we didn't want a police-styled action to take back the hallways. It would be a well-researched, planned approach designed to create a better environment through intervention and teaching kids social competency. That's where my special education background became useful because I was trained to teach social competency long term in order to create a civil environment."

For references, Gottlieb said they leaned upon the teachings of Hill Walker, a respected University of Oregon professor who designed a 'pro-social' method of identifying problem children at an early age, along with a plan for bumping them off the destructive path they're traveling. By studying the children's home atmosphere, Gottlieb says Walker can generally tell at age five if a child is destined to commit a felony by age 17. This is accomplished by scrutinizing five aspects of their family life, which they used by applying the school as 'family' and the teachers as 'parents.' Gottlieb relates them as:

- The family practices consistent discipline offered without embarrassment or coercion, given in a positive manner that avoids the "wait until your father comes home" type threats. It also promotes consistent expectations in a nonhumiliating, nonnagging way.

- The family monitors the children to know where they are and what's going on in their lives. "If a parent is suspicious of something in a teenager's room, they check without being invasive. To take this theory into Deerfield, there shouldn't be a hallway where the teacher's can't walk through," Gottlieb says.

- The parents practice positive reinforcement. "Tell them what they are doing right as opposed to just correcting them when they are wrong." Thanking kids for doing a good job and rewarding them for good behavior.

- The parents stay involved. "Teachers should talk to the students about things outside of academics. They should get to know them as people."

- The family should practice problem solving. Teaching kids to identify problems and developing a way of reacting using alternate means. Stay close to the kids during this process to evaluate how it's working out.

As detailed in Chapter 5, the faculty and administratively developed First Class program at Deerfield was a rousing success almost from day one. Gottlieb recalls some dissident teachers tempering the achievements around the edges, but said their protests were mostly silent. "There was a strong groundswell to do this, and we appealed to their sense of teamwork. The question among them was, 'Did I become a high school teacher to teach behavior?' My answer was, 'Yes! That is part of it.' It worked out because the hard-line, punitive-types liked First Class because it got the teachers who generally avoided problems to participate. The non-hard line types liked it because it created a kinder and gentler spirit among the punitive group. And the reaction of the students was consistent with research that reveals that if students feel they are disliked by their teachers, they won't learn as much. If they feel liked and respected, they will learn more."

Which brings us to the purpose of this chapter. We know that First Class had an overwhelming positive effect upon the general student body at Deerfield, Carl Sandburg, and Mundelein, but how did it play in "The Cage"?

"Very positively!" Gottlieb recalls. "Sure, these kids would be the first to reject it at inception because they feel more at risk in being rejected themselves. They are more leery of everything because they've been rejected all their lives. Their attitude was 'This is a bunch of BS. Teachers are jerks! We'll see who really cares.' I had a good relationship with them, and they knew I was into it, so they tempered their reaction to my face, but their initial suspicious attitudes were to be expected. Once we got over that, First Class was even more successful with my kids. The staff made a conscious decision to help the more troubled youths learn problem solving. Before First Class, a lot of people felt my kids didn't belong in the cafeteria or the halls. The feeling was, 'Why are they on the loose?' The new, First Class way of thinking opened the faculty up to understanding and not being afraid of them. Plus, the faculty was given additional training in how to deal with such kids.

"The question was, over the course of the year, would it continue to build and get better? It did. Teachers who once told me, 'That kid will never be in my class again!' were now saying, 'Let's talk about bringing him back.' The teachers wanted to try to work it out because we had created a more humanistic environment. It was no longer custodial. So, with the teachers being more willing to accept and experiment, it enabled my students to get out into the school a little more. Of course, some of my kids thought it was a trick. There's no panacea. But by and large, things got significantly better for them."

Another problem with bringing First Class to special needs students is the perception that giving students more influence over their behavior in a humanistic environment is akin to the old cliché of giving inmates control of the prison. Gottlieb insists that this isn't the case.

"It absolutely didn't result in that kind of reaction. First Class doesn't create a more permissive environment. There is actually an increased vigilance toward promoting positive intervention. The students didn't have it easier. Before, the attitude was 'That's a kid out of The Cage. I better not mess with them.' After First Class, it was accepted that every staff member would have the right to deal with every kid, including my kids. It goes back to Hill Walker's belief in creating a very clear understanding of discipline and expectations that are practiced consistently by the entire 'family.'

"If there was a more permissive environment, my kids would have definitely taken advantage of it, and they would have been much worse. Instead, there were clearer understandings and more skills among the faculty. As a result, my kids were much better."

As Deerfield's First Class program progressed, Gottlieb discovered that he was increasingly able to succeed at his original, pre-First Class goal of mainstreaming his students back into the regular school day. Experiments with allowing them to go to the cafeteria, and placing them in high-level art and music classes to shape and focus natural abilities, more times than not proved to be successful. "There were increased instances of the art teachers incorporating my kids into the studio arts program without having them meet all the normal prerequisites. If the students had the talent, they would be allowed to take these advanced classes. Similarly, I recall that the basketball coach on a number of occasions worked with the Special Needs students to keep them on the team, even in the face of crazy parents who interfered and gave the coach hell. Before First Class, the coach would have thrown the kid off the team to avoid all that, but afterward there was a marked change."

As a result of these and other examples, there was a dramatic lessening of tension between the "Sweat Hogs" and the faculty.

"The kids would tell me, 'Hey, I think the teachers are mellowing out. They're not as big a jerks as they used to be.' The reason was that all people respond to being treated with respect. My kids were no different."

Interestingly enough, Gottlieb noted that it wasn't just his problem children that were benefiting from this new faculty attitude. "Everybody can benefit from somebody reaching out and finding their strengths. Schools should do that for everybody."

The downside to all this is the fact that a First Class program cannot prevent the explosion of troubled children coming into the high school system each autumn. "Gradually, over the years, we've seen an exponential growth of Special Needs kids and those being identified as having behavior disorders. Our society is not creating a better environment for our youth. Schools are accepting the responsibility more and doing a better job at trying to correct this, but their numbers aren't getting fewer. We never anticipated that it would. There are profound societal factors at work with these students, and First Class can be a very impatient concept for them at times. What we have been able to do is create a sense of belonging for those who are different. There's a greater willingness to support these kids and to take ownership of all the students. They are not just 'my kids' anymore. They are everybody's. I've seen a big increase in the Special Education students participating in sports, clubs, and other after-school activities since First Class. And there's been a more humanistic approach by the faculty and administrators to go the extra mile before putting a child out of school. They've backed away from the concept of zero tolerance a bit."

Unfortunately, as Gottlieb noted, society is producing more and more troubled children. And despite First Class trained teachers bending over backward to avoid giving up on their problem children, increasing numbers are getting "put out." When that happens in the Deerfield area, they all end up with Bob Gottlieb. In 1992, Gottlieb became the principal of North Shore Academy, a school consisting entirely of teenagers kicked out of special needs classes.

"This is a therapeutic school for the profoundly emotionally disturbed," Gottlieb explains. "These are not funny oddballs like on *Welcome Back Kotter*. That's a television show. That's not who shows up at my door."

The disturbed kids who do show up ban together to create an intense atmosphere. Aside from the specifically trained Special Education teachers, there are ten psychologists on staff along with an assortment of social workers charged with handling and healing the school's 120 students. The classes themselves usually consist of three adults and ten students, making for a more interactive student/teacher ratio. The course subjects are heavily intertwined with therapy, as in music, drama, and art. The behavior guidelines are tightly enforced. "The rules in a therapeutic high school are not fuzzy. We'd die if they were. But we deliver them in a softer, caring tone of voice," Gottlieb says.

Even with the no-nonsense approach, the school leans heavily upon the First Class ideals Gottlieb brought with him from Deerfield. "We have the same concept as First Class, only more so. We don't call it First Class. We call it 'The Circle of Courage.' It's based upon the book *Reclaiming Youth at Risk* by Martin Brokenleg, Larry

Brendtro, and Steve Van Bockern. It's about the Black Hills seminars held on the South Dakota Sioux Reservation. The themes they instill involve belonging, independence, mastery, and generosity. We filter all our policies through these ideals, handling one per quarter."

As with the other schools, North Shore stages events and contests around their Circle of Courage that involve such things as student-made posters, mosaics, and art. "It is very prevalent in the culture of our school. We have hundreds of Circle of Courage activities like recycling efforts, visiting preschools and senior citizen centers, breakfasts with the faculty, etc. I've even brought a climbing wall into the gym for the students to help each other descend.

"Not every aspect of First Class works with my kids. Every environment has to adjust its level of expectations. The whole concept requires it to be individualized to each community. You can't take First Class and use it as a cookbook in another school. If you do that, its chances of working are very slim. At Deerfield, the idea was to treat each other with respect. At North Shore, we want the kids to follow staff directives within a one-minute time frame. We also need to have more follow through and resiliency. What's important everywhere is for the faculty of each school to get solidly behind it.

"I think every successful school is doing First Class in one way or another. There's an effort to take more of a humanistic approach to students and teach them social consciousness. Kids learn more in these environments."

In essence, to answer the question posed at the top, programs like First Class that are infused with respect and dignity work across the board with all students—even the Sweat Hogs.

EPILOGUE

A NEW GENERATION
CARRIES THE BATON

Prior to the grassroots First Class movement at Mundelein, the oddly named Illinois school was already nationally known for a rather strange accomplishment. A "Bill Nye the Science Guy" type teacher had designed and constructed what was essentially a Y2K shop class to end all shop classes. Over the years, starting well into Y1K, Mundelein "technology" teacher Jim Jackson and his students built and flew four airplanes—all without incident. The noteworthy, if somewhat bizarre, accomplishment spawned from a rare high school-level aviation class has earned Jackson a host of Teacher-of-the-Year awards, along with a summons to the White House.

Granted, few things can match the adrenaline rush—and flop sweat fear—of soaring over the aptly named Windy City inside an aircraft built by Fonzie and his gang down in shop. Nevertheless, the more grounded First Class movement has seized the torch and taken over as Mundelein's claim to fame. The students griping about a "homecoming from hell" outside French class in 1996 helped power an educational groundswell that will eventually touch millions of impressionable children from Key West, Florida to Fairbanks, Alaska, with side trips to Hawaii and Guam. Even Jackson and his high flying Fonzies haven't taken their creation that far. (Although they did go to the Arctic Circle!)

In their little corner of the world, Karen Royer, John Ahlgrim, John Davis, Tee Newbrough, and the much-mentioned Mundelein Gang of Nine—with a big assist from rival school honcho John Scornavacco—not only created, but lived out what can now be christened as the blueprint for bottom-up character education in our nation's schools.

"I went back for the first day this year and I saw a whole bunch of people with tie-dye shirts on," recent graduate Jennifer Bouteille says. "I went to go look at what club these people belonged to, and sure enough the school had provided shirts for all the First Class leaders. It made me feel so good to know that all the hard work that was put in my freshman year was still being used, and that the school was getting even more involved."

Bravo, Mundelein. Keep your chins up, language clean, assemblies hopping, noses to the educational grindstone, and personal integrity tip-top, but watch out for low-flying aircraft!

On a beautiful spring day in 1999, 1,700 Mundelein High School students marched out to the football field to send a no-nonsense message to the rest of the nation about the importance of teaching teenagers the concept of right and wrong. Is anybody listening? (Credit—Jim Jackson and Jack Pawlowski)

PART 3

OPINIONS, REPORTS, FACTS, AND RESOURCES

20 TROUBLING FACTS

ABOUT AMERICAN

EDUCATION

STUDENT PERFORMANCE

1. American 12th graders rank 19th out of 21 industrialized countries in mathematics achievement and 16th out of 21 nations in science. Our advanced physics students rank dead last.

2. Since 1983, over 10 million Americans have reached the 12th grade without having learned to read at a basic level. Over 20 million have reached their senior year unable to do basic math. Almost 25 million have reached 12th grade not knowing the essentials of U.S. history.

3. In the same period, over 6 million Americans dropped out of high school altogether. In 1996, 44% of Hispanic immigrants aged 16–24 were not in school and did not hold a diploma.

4. In the fourth grade, 77% of children in urban high-poverty schools are reading "below basic" on the National Assessment of Educational Progress (NAEP).

5. Currently, average black and Hispanic 17-year-old children have NAEP scores in math, science, reading, and writing that are equivalent to average white 13-year-old children.

School Spending and Use of Resources

6. Average per-pupil spending in U.S. public schools rose 212% from 1960 to 1995 in real (i.e., inflation-adjusted) dollars.

7. In 1960, for every U.S. public school teacher there were approximately 26 students enrolled in the schools. In 1995, there were 17.

8. In 1994, fewer than 50% of the personnel employed by U.S. public schools were teachers.

9. The average salary of U.S. public school teachers rose 45% in real dollars from 1960 to 1995.

Readiness for College and Work

10. In 1995, nearly 30% of first-time college freshmen enrolled in at least one remedial course and 80% of all public four-year universities offered remedial courses.

11. According to U.S. manufacturers, 40% of all 17-year-olds do not have the math skills and 60% lack the reading skills to hold down a production job at a manufacturing company.

12. 76% of college professors and 63% of employers believe that "a high school diploma is no guarantee that the typical student has learned the basics."

Teacher Quality

13. Only 38% of U.S. public school teachers majored in an academic subject in college.

14. 40% of public high school science teachers have neither an undergraduate major nor minor in their main teaching field and 34% of public high school math teachers did not major or minor in math or related fields.

15. Only one in five teachers feels well prepared to teach to high academic standards.

STUDENT BEHAVIOR

16. In 1996, 64% of high school seniors reported doing less than one hour of homework per night.

17. 57% of public schools reported moderate to serious discipline problems in the 1996–97 school year.

THE FEDERAL ROLE

18. In Florida, it takes six times as many people to administer a federal education dollar as a state dollar: 297 state employees are responsible for $1 billion in federal funds while 374 employees oversee $7 billion in state funds.

19. In Arizona, 45% of the staff of the state education department is responsible for managing federal programs that account for 6 percent of the state's education spending.

20. After spending $118 billion since 1965 on Title I, the federal government's largest K-12 program, evaluations conclude that the "program has been unable to lift [the] academic level of poor students."

Reprinted by permission from Empower America (www.empower.com).

SOURCE NOTES

1. *Pursuing Excellence: A Study of U.S. Twelfth-Grade Mathematics and Science Achievement in International Context* (Washington, DC: U.S. Department of Education, National Center for Education Statistics, February 1998).

2. *A Nation Still at Risk: An Education Manifesto* (Washington, DC: April 30, 1998) (see www.edexcellence.net.)

3. *Ibid.*

4. *Quality Counts '98: The Urban Challenge* (Washington, DC: Editorial Projects in Education, January 8, 1998).

5. Larry Stedman, "An Assessment of the Contemporary Debate over U.S. Achievement," in *Brookings Papers on Education Policy 1998* (Washington, DC: The Brookings Institution, 1998).

6. *Digest of Education Statistics 1997*, table 39.

7. *Digest of Education Statistics 1997*, figure 8.

8. Organization for Economic Cooperation and Development (OECD), *Education at a Glance: OECD Indicators* (Paris, OECD, 1995), table p31.

9. *Digest of Education Statistics 1997*, table 39.

10. David W. Breneman, "Remediation in Higher Education: Its Extent and Cost," in *Brookings Papers on Education Policy 1998* (Washington, DC: The Brookings Institution, 1998).

11. *Education and Training for America's Future* (Washington, DC: National Association of Manufacturers, January 1998).

12. *Reality Check* (New York: Public Agenda, January 1998).

13. *Teacher Quality: A Report on the Preparation and Qualifications of Public School Teachers* (Washington, DC: U.S. Department of Education, National Center for Education Statistics, January 1999).

14. *America's Teachers: Profile of a Profession, 1993–1994* (Washington, DC: U.S. Department of Education, National Center for Education Statistics, July 1997).

15. *Teacher Quality: A Report on the Preparation and Qualifications of Public School Teachers* (Washington, DC: U.S. Department of Education, National Center for Education Statistics, January 1999).

16. *Digest of Education Statistics 1997.*

17. Marci Kanstoroom and Chester E. Finn, Jr., eds., *New Directions: Federal Education Policy in the Twenty-First Century* (Washington, DC: Thomas B. Fordham Foundation, March 1999).

18. *Prospects for Reform: The State of American Education and the Federal Role* (Washington, DC: U.S. Senate Budget Committee Task Force on Education, 1998).

19. Lisa Graham Keegan, "Back Off, Washington," in Marci Kanstoroom and Chester E. Finn, Jr., eds., *New Directions: Federal Education Policy in the Twenty-First Century* (Washington, DC: Thomas B. Fordham Foundation, March 1999).

20. Ralph Frammolino, "Title I's $118 Billion Fails to Close Gap," *Los Angeles Times*, January 17, 1999.

Printed by permission from Empower America, *www.empower.com*

Empower America

1701 Pennsylvania Avenue, NW, Suite 900

Washington, DC 20006

phone: (202) 452-8200

fax: (202) 833-0388

U.S. GOVERNMENT GRANTS AND STATE REPORTS

THE PARTNERSHIPS IN CHARACTER EDUCATION PILOT PROJECTS PROGRAM FROM THE U.S. DEPARTMENT OF EDUCATION

Program Information:

The Partnerships in Character Education Pilot Projects Program is authorized under Title X, Part A, Section 10103 of the Elementary and Secondary Education Act as amended. Part A is the Fund for the Improvement of Education (FIE).

The Secretary may make a total of 10 grants annually to state educational agencies (SEA) in partnership with one or more local educational agencies (LEA). Each state is limited to a total of 1 million dollars over a period of no more than five years. The state may retain no more than 30 percent of the funds; the remainder must be given to the LEAs. The Department of Education has funded 37 states.

Parents, students, and community members, including private and nonprofit organizations, can participate in the design and administration of the projects. The projects will help states work with school districts to develop curriculum materials, provide teacher training, involve parents in character education, and integrate character education into the curriculum. Each project will design activities to incorporate six elements of character—caring, civic virtue and citizenship, justice and fairness, respect, responsibility, and trustworthiness. Projects may add other elements of character deemed appropriate by the members of the partnership. Each project must also establish a clearinghouse for the distribution of materials and information about character education and include an evaluation designed to determine the success toward reducing discipline problems, and improving student grades, participation in extracurricular activities, and parent and community involvement.

*   *   *

The following are reports, plans, and mission statements from a selection of states around the nation that have implemented, or are planning to implement, The Partnerships in Character Education Pilot Projects Program.

ARIZONA

CHARACTER EDUCATION COMMISSION
VISION, MISSION, VALUES AND GUIDING PRINCIPLES
REVISED – DECEMBER 13, 1999

Vision

Arizona will be recognized and respected nationally as a model state by providing voluntary education and training on the core values of trustworthiness, respect, responsibility, fairness, caring and citizenship to educators, leaders of youth nonprofit organizations and children in Arizona. This will be made possible through collaborations with businesses; educators; community organizations; the State of Arizona; state and local agencies that deal with parents and youth; Sovereign Nations; all other levels of government; youth sports programs; and all stakeholders that work with youth.

Mission

The Character Education Commission provides leadership to the state and local communities and in collaboration with the Arizona Character Education Foundation will:

Implement and promote an effective character education program to be offered in Arizona.

Key Strategies

- To provide character education training to Arizona educators and youth nonprofit organizations, sectarian and nonsectarian, at no charge by collaborating with the Arizona Character Education Foundation and all other nonprofit organizations.

- To promote community involvement in character education.

- To raise the awareness of the importance of character education through participation in national and local awareness campaigns.

- To recognize those youth who exemplify exceptional character.

- To lay a foundation for the long-term sustainability of character education in Arizona by collaborating with the Arizona Character Education Foundation.

- To recognize those educators and leaders who excel in character education.

- To "memorialize" the media and strongly encourage the media to report about positive youth role models and youth activities.

- To challenge everyone in the community to recognize that youth are assets to the community.

- Instill self-confidence in our youth.

- Advocate for youth and model our program.

- Understand the program and utilize contacts to further the character education efforts in Arizona.

VALUES AND GUIDING PRINCIPLES

1. We value young people and recognize they are our future leaders.
2. We value youth as assets to our community.
3. We value that character training of children has taken on a new sense of urgency as violence by and against youth threatens the

physical and psychological well-being of the people in Arizona and the United States.

4. We value that children need strong and constructive guidance from their families and their communities, including schools, youth organizations, and civic groups.

5. We value educators, youth community organizations, positive peer mentors, and youth leaders for the impact they have on our children.

6. We value character education that instills core values of trustworthiness, respect, responsibility, fairness, caring, and citizenship in all citizens.

THE ARIZONA CHARACTER EDUCATION BALLOT DRIVE NOVEMBER 2000
15-154.01 CHARACTER EDUCATION MATCHING GRANT PROGRAM

A. Any public or charter school that teaches a character education curriculum pursuant to section 15-719 is eligible for a state-matching grant of up to one thousand five hundred dollars annually. The school shall provide matching monies from any lawful source.

B. The character education program shall be an age-specific, stand-alone character education curriculum with the following elements:

1. Applicable definitions for character qualities that include at least five of the following attributes:

(a) attentiveness.

(b) caring.

(c) citizenship.

(d) compassion.

(e) diligence.

(f) discernment.

(g) forgiveness.

(h) generosity.

(i) gratefulness.

(j) initiative.

(k) orderliness.

(l) respect.

(m) responsibility.

(n) sincerity.

(o) trustworthiness.

(p) virtue.

(q) wisdom.

2. Activities that provide a forum for practical application and an environment in which character-related behavior is identified, recognized, and reinforced such as literature or visual media presentations or discussion of character values as they relate to a specific story.

3. Stories from the lives of our nation's leaders, where character qualities are demonstrated.

4. Mentors or teachers who demonstrate the character qualities defined in the lessons presented.

5. Provides mentor and teacher training for praising students who demonstrate specific character qualities.

6. Provides a precourse and postcourse survey of parents, teachers, and students on their assessment of the program.

C. The State Department of Education shall administer the program and distribute the state matching grant monies.

D. The State Department of Education shall apply for all applicable character education grants from the federal government.

E. The program established by this section ends on July 1, 2010 pursuant to section 41-3102.

MARYLAND

MARYLAND STATE DEPARTMENT OF EDUCATION CHARACTER EDUCATION INITIATIVE RESULTS

Goal:

To create safe and orderly schools, and prevent youth violence, drug use and gangs by promoting honesty, fairness, trustworthiness, respect, and responsibility.

Background:

Implemented in 1997, these results evaluate the first year of implementation in 109 schools in five Maryland jurisdictions.

Summary:

Improvements on all perceptions of student behavior.

Results:

Survey of Student Behavior in Schools with Character Education (Ranking scale: 1 = Strongly Disagree, 5 = Strongly Agree)

SURVEY STATEMENT	BASELINE AFTER AVERAGE	YEAR 1	CHANGE
When students do something hurtful they apologize and try to make up for it.	2.48	2.95	+.47
Students solve conflicts without fighting, insults or threats.	2.51	2.97	+.46
Students respect others' personal property.	3.14	3.59	+.45
Students treat classmates and schoolmates with respect.	3.09	3.53	+.44
Students feel they can talk to their teachers about things that are bothering them.	3.23	3.66	+.43
Students refrain from put-downs.	2.46	2.88	+.42
Older students are kind to younger students.	2.99	3.40	+.41
Students refrain from picking on others because they are different.	2.68	3.08	+.40

Source: Gary Skaggs, Evaluation of the Maryland Partnership in Character Education Year One Report, West Mesa Associates, Inc. The statistics above come from a survey, which was administered to 17,770 administrators, students, teachers, parents, and support staff in all 109 participating schools.

MOTON ELEMENTARY SCHOOL
EASTON, MARYLAND
CHARACTER EDUCATION SUMMARY OF RESULTS

	SEPT. 1997	SEPT. 1998
Discipline problem:		
Insubordination and Disrespect	700	423
Classroom Disruption	115	36

NEW MEXICO

BEL AIRE ELEMENTARY SCHOOL
ALBUQUERQUE
CHARACTER EDUCATION RESULTS

Goal:

To integrate character education into new and existing programs and to encourage young people and their parents to adopt and model trustworthiness, respect, responsibility, fairness, caring, and citizenship.

Background:

Implemented in 1994, these results evaluate the first year of implementation in the Bel Aire Elementary School.

Summary:

Improvements on all perceptions of student behavior.

Results:

During September, 1993, the school reported:

    64 official reprimands for bad behavior

    25 fights

    Four months after systematically teaching ethical concepts with consistent language, the results were:

    17 official reprimands

    6 fights

In May 1996, just one year after receiving funding for its Character Counts initiative, 97 percent of school principals at Albuquerque's 117 public schools agreed to include character education in school curricula.

In gang-plagued Garfield Middle School, during the first 20 days of the school year (before implementing character education), they recorded 91 incidents of physical violence among its 570 students. The next year, 26 such incidents were reported in the same time period.

CALIFORNIA

CALIFORNIA PARTNERSHIPS IN CHARACTER EDUCATION
CHARACTER EDUCATION RESULTS

Goal:

To create multiple school models for character education in California.

Background:

Implemented in 10 schools (five elementary, three middle and two junior high) in California. It was implemented in five elementary schools first, then followed by middle schools in the third year of the project.

Summary of Results:

School suspensions down.

Parents, staff, and students feel their school is a safer place.

Student attendance is up.

Staff, parents, and student attitudes about schools improved.

School community speaks a common character language.

Character is a visible part of school climate.

Preliminary findings to date indicated no statistical significant impact on student achievement as gauged by standardized test scores.

Other Results:

STUDENT SUSPENSIONS (COMBINED FOR THREE SCHOOLS*)

1995-96	1996-97	1997-98	1998-99
279	223	196	126

*These schools provided four years of data. All other schools provided less than four years, however achieved excellent results.

CALIFORNIA CHARACTER EDUCATION PILOT PROGRAM
"COMMUNITIES AND SCHOOLS OF CHARACTER"

Overview of Project:

- California's program was funded by the United States Department of Education for a four-year pilot program. The goal of the program was to plan and develop models for character education. The California Department of Education collaborated with the Sacramento County Office of Education.

- Five elementary schools started the project. In the third year of the project, five middle schools joined. Because the schools were located in rural, suburban, and urban environments, every school customized its own character education program.

- The pilot schools were in very different places when the project began. Some of the schools participating in the grant are from districts that had district-wide character education plans and support systems in place. Other schools pioneered character education in their districts.

- The Six Elements were:
    Caring
    Citizenship
    Civic Virtue
    Justice and Fairness
    Respect
    Responsibility and Trustworthiness

- Model Project Schools
    Al Tahoe Elementary School; Lake Tahoe Unified School District (El Dorado County)
    Arbuckle Elementary School; Pierce Joint Unified School District (Colusa County)
    Dry Creek Elementary School; Rio Linda Union School District (Sacramento County)
    Fern Bacon Middle School; Sacramento City Unified School District (Sacramento County)
    Lloyd G. Johnson Junior High School; Pierce Joint Unified School District (Colusa County)

Nicholas Elementary School; Sacramento City Unified School District (Sacramento County)

Rio Linda Junior High School; Grant Joint Union High School District (Sacramento County)

Skycrest Elementary School; San Juan Unified School District (Sacramento County)

South Tahoe Middle School; Lake Tahoe Unified School District (El Dorado County)

Will Rogers Middle School; San Juan Unified School District (Sacramento County)

Implementation

Year One

Served as a baseline year. The five elementary schools involved at that time used that year to address:

Needs, research, and writings on character education

Program pilots currently in existence

Curricula that address the topic

Varied resources and instructional strategies

Issues related to school environment

Working with students, parents, and community members

School/Community Education

Year Two

The year of implementation for the elementary schools

Staff development and on-site implementation continued

Five middle schools whose students were being fed from the elementary schools with the existing Character Education Program were recruited to join the project at the beginning of the third year

Year Three

Focused on dissemination of information about the project's progress

Middle schools began their staff development and on-site training

The elementary schools continued from year two

Year Four

The pilot elementary schools continued

The middle schools began project implementation

School Data

- The elementary school students realized a 6.76-point improvement in the second/third graders' reading scores and a 12.92-point increase in their math scores.

- On a scale of 1 to 5 (5 being very positive impact) participants, including parents, teachers, students, and administrators, felt that character education's impact on their school was a 4.48.

- School climate was ranked as the top area of the school impacted.

- All five of the middle schools had their suspensions decrease during their two years in the project.

- Arbuckle elementary school suspensions went down from 167 in 1995-96, to 88 in 1998-99.

- Fern Bacon Middle School went from 470 suspensions (1996-97) to 204 suspensions (1998-99).

- Rio Linda Jr. High School went from 621 suspensions (1997-98) to 389 suspensions (1998-99).

- Eight of the 10 schools saw an increase in student attendance over the years.

- Lloyd Johnson Jr. High School had an 87% attendance rating in 1996-97, and increased to 96% in 1998-99.

Summary of School Results

- School suspensions went down.

- Parents, staff, and students feel their school is a safer place.

- Student attendance went up.

- Staff, parents', and students' attitudes about schools improved.

- School community speaks a common character language.

- Character is a visible part of school climate.

IOWA

IOWA PARTNERSHIPS IN CHARACTER EDUCATION
CHARACTER EDUCATION RESULTS

Goal:

To promote character education throughout the state of Iowa. By the year 2001, the Iowa Department of Education will have developed an approach to school improvement consistent with the goals of the national Goals 2000 program, which integrates the Character Education Learning Community Model as an integral part of the schools and process.

Background:

To date, over 12,500 students are involved in the program (5th, 8th, and 11th graders).

Summary of Results:

A final report has not been developed. However, data from the resiliency survey show improvement from 2.95 to 3.2. They directly correlate this to the increased awareness of traits of respect, trust, and responsibility.

SOUTH DAKOTA

SOUTH DAKOTA CHARACTER EDUCATION PROGRAM
CHARACTER EDUCATION RESULTS

Summary of Results:

	BASELINE	AFTER 1 YEAR OF CHARACTER EDUCATION
Cheated on an exam	57%	53%
Used physical force against someone	50%	34%
Told a lie to a parent	83%	73%
Drank alcoholic beverages	50%	38%
Used an illegal drug	23%	18%
Damaged or vandalized property	26%	17%
Took something without paying	35%	23%

(7,496 surveys were returned in 1998; 6,156 were returned in 1999)

NEW JERSEY

NEW JERSEY CHARACTER EDUCATION PARTNERSHIP (NJCEP) INITIATIVE

Initiative Overview:

In her State-of-the-State message in January 2000, former Republican Governor Christine Todd Whitman announced a new statewide character education initiative, titled the New Jersey Character Education Partnership (NJCEP). The purpose of this four-year initiative is to assist public school educators to adopt validated character education programs that will meet the developmental needs of students throughout New Jersey by promoting pro-social student behaviors and creating a caring, disciplined school climate conducive to learning. A dedicated state aid line item in the Governor's fiscal year 2001 budget provides $4.75 million to public school districts and approved charter schools to be devoted to character education program development and implementation during the 2000-2001 school year. The Department of Education is administering the initiative and is supporting implementation of character education programs through professional development and information networking.

State Aid Funding and Application Process:

During the first year of the project, every school district and charter school is receiving a minimum of $4,000 in state aid to implement a character education program in at least one school building. School districts with enrollments greater than 1,358 students receive additional funds. The aid for these districts is based upon $2.945 per resident student. If a district receives more than sufficient funds to implement a program in one building, the use of the additional funds will be restricted for use in implementing character education programs in other buildings or for maintaining or expanding existing character education programs.

School districts and charter schools are required to submit a short application to the department to choose among a limited number of Character Education Programs of Merit, or districts may choose other programs if they have adequate rationale for their choice. Information regarding the Character Education Programs of Merit Profile Directory may be received by contacting the office below.

State aid allocations will be mailed to districts and charter schools in late July.

For More Information:

For more information about the New Jersey Character Education Partnership (NJCEP), visit the department's web site at http://www. state.nj.us/education or contact the New Jersey Department of Education, Division of Student Services, Office of Educational Support Services and Interagency Initiatives, 100 River View Plaza, Trenton, New Jersey 08625-0500, Gloria Hancock, Director, Telephone: (609) 292-5935, Fax number: (609) 633-9655.

Summary of the Federal Grant:

The New Jersey Department of Education has a seven-year history of innovative and sustained program activity promoting the development of character and values education in the state's schools. An earlier Governor's initiative, Developing Character and Values in New Jersey Students, launched program and policy activity in more than half of the state's 596 school districts, supported by professional development and networking opportunities and four department publications. The effort has been recognized by local and state media such as the *Newark Star Ledger*, as well as the *New York Times* and *Philadelphia Inquirer*.

The New Jersey Character Education Pilot Program funded for four years by the U.S. Department of Education under the Improving America's Schools Act, Partnerships in Character Education Pilot Projects grant program, involves a partnership with the State's largest school system, the Newark Public Schools, and the Newark Do Something Fund. The pilot project will create a demonstration project of national significance while allowing all of the state's schools to become partners with the state in developing and refining character education programs and strategies. Specifically, the department will implement the following plan:

Working in partnership with the Newark School District, and a community development agency, the Newark Do Something Fund, the New Jersey Department of Education will develop an urban pilot project with the following components: Infusion of character education through a curriculum renewal process grounded in the state's Core Curriculum Content Standards and implemented in all 54 public schools in Newark with grades K-8; refinement and implementation of a school/community service learning and school climate change program organized by the Newark Do Something Fund which is already operating in 12 Newark middle schools and will be expanded to all middle schools in the district. Additionally, the proposal details a plan to test the replicability of the project model through two identified and committed collaborating partners, the Jersey City and Paterson School Districts, and to evaluate all aspects of the project utilizing the services of an external contractor to assure objectivity.

The second part of the plan is the formation of the New Jersey Character Education Network, which will provide a larger scale of experimentation with a range of character education strategies, procedures, and program designs. Because it will be a resource for any New Jersey public or private school that wants to join, it will function more inclusively than the Newark demonstration project. The network will also provide a forum for sharing the results of worthy character education efforts from New Jersey and elsewhere.

The establishment of a character education clearinghouse function, professional development and conferencing opportunities, planned publications, and the support of the national Character Education Partnership will facilitate and enhance the ability of the department to provide technical assistance and disseminate project outcomes.

NINE STATES RECEIVE CHARACTER EDUCATION GRANTS PRESS RELEASE

U.S. Secretary of Education Richard W. Riley announced today that nine states have received a total of $2.5 million in grants to form partnerships with local school districts and communities to help youth incorporate good citizenship into their education.

"Good citizenship, compassion and respect for others are qualities just as important as learning to high standards in math, science and reading," Riley said, "and school is where most young people spend most of their time outside the home. With these grants, schools and communities can reinforce parents in helping students learn to make good choices and be positive members of society throughout their lives."

Under the Partnerships in Character Education Pilot Projects Program, the grantees will launch partnerships with one or more local school districts to establish character education programs for youth.

Parents, students, and other community members, including private and nonprofit organizations, can participate in the design and administration of programs. The character education partnerships will help states work with school districts to develop curriculum materials, provide teacher training, gauge and build community consensus on common values, involve parents in character education, and integrate character education into the curriculum.

The projects will be evaluated to determine their success toward reducing discipline problems and improving student grades, increasing participation in extracurricular activities, and strengthening parent and community involvement. States are also asked to establish a clearinghouse for the distribution of materials and information about character education.

The grantees were selected from among 15 eligible applicants.

The Partnerships in Character Education Pilot Projects Program is authorized under Title X, Part A, Section 10103 of the Improving America's School Act (P.L. 203-382).

* * *

Following are grant amounts and contacts made in 1999-2000.

District of Columbia Public Schools: $271,731
  Contact: Georgia A. Booker (202) 442-5599
Idaho State Department of Education: $250,000
  Contact: Karen Fraley (208) 332-6928
Maine Department of Education: $400,000
  Contact: Susan Corrente (207) 287-3272
Massachusetts Department of Education: $198,195
  Contact: Francis Kane (781) 338-3900
Michigan Department of Education: $314,723
  Contact: Peter Bunton (517) 373-7247
Nebraska Department of Education: $183,183
  Contact: John LeFeber (402) 471-2449
Rhode Island Department of Elementary and Secondary Education: $334,578
  Contact: Linda N. Greenwood (401) 222-4600
Tennessee Department of Education: $250,000
  Contact: Bruce Opie (615) 532-6288
Virginia Department of Education: $333,333
  Contact: Marsha E. Owens (804) 225-2928

MUNDELEIN AND DEERFIELD HIGH SCHOOLS FACTS, INFORMATION, AND MEMOS

This is how Mundelein High School presents itself on its web page (http://www.mhslake.net/default.htm):

Mundelein High School District #120
1350 West Hawley Street
Mundelein, Illinois 60060
847-949-2200

Mundelein is 41.8 miles NW of Chicago—about a 57-minute drive. Mundelein High School, located in Mundelein, Illinois, is home to 1,710 high school students and 260 faculty and staff. Our school is on the cutting edge of learning technologies and innovative teaching practices. We are a Block 4 School. At Mundelein, we prepare our students for the 21st century. We are a Blue Ribbon School.

MHS has 600 computers connected to the Internet. We have 18 computer labs and Internet-accessible computers in every classroom. We are one of the first in Illinois to operate a building-wide Gigabit

Ethernet network, with 100 megabit connections to every classroom computer. We operate one of the Midwest's first building-wide digital video-on-demand video networks, with 32″ TVs in every classroom.

MUNDELEIN HIGH SCHOOL

MHS TODAY

The School

Mundelein High School is a comprehensive high school which serves the needs of all residents of the Mundelein community. The district's 1,740 students come from a 36-square-mile area.

The school has a strong, traditional academic program. Approximately 50% to 60% of the senior class take the American College Test (ACT) each year, and more than 85% of Mundelein High School graduates continue their education at institutions of advanced training.

The school offers special education services to all eligible students and The Lake County High Schools Technology Campus offers training programs in such subjects as health, child care, autobody repair, and graphics.

MHS is the only school in the state, and possibly the nation, to boast an Aviation Technology Program that has constructed four airplanes.

MHS is situated on a 40-acre campus that includes tennis courts, four gymnasiums, an indoor Olympic-sized pool, and football and soccer fields. The original building includes 50 classrooms along with offices for pupil personnel services, business and operations, and administration. The original building also houses the cafeteria, auditorium, main gymnasium, and music wing. Two building additions include an additional 20 classrooms, a state-of-the-art foreign language laboratory with satellite reception for European programming, a natatorium, and a gymnasium with an elevated running track. A 1996 building and remodeling referendum for $12.5 million was used to renovate science and math classrooms in the original building and construct a wing which houses business education and English classes in 20 first-floor classrooms and a Media Center with computer labs on the second floor.

Students participate in a variety of extracurricular activities and clubs, including foreign language clubs, newspaper, yearbook, literary magazine, forensics, student government, plays, and musicals. The school has three bands, three choirs, and 19 interscholastic sports, plus intramural sports.

*   *   *

Random thoughts on First Class from Mundelein students in teacher Diane VonderHaar's 2000-2001 journalism class:

"So far, I like my First Class. I enjoy my leader's lessons, and the discussions we talk about. As a new student, I was kind of hesitant about First Class, now I talk aloud and express my thoughts."

———

"First Class is a good way to express your opinions on controversial topics such as abortion, without feeling like you are going to offend someone."

———

"First Class is a good idea, but students need to agree. If students have negative opinions of the program, they won't participate. Discussions are often not very good because no one wants to share their ideas with the group. If student involvement was increased, the school would benefit from the program more."

———

"First Class is a great way for students to get together and talk about situations occurring in school. (It's a) great program that has helped many students become aware of situations in and out of school."

———

"First Class helps students get to know other cultures outside their own."

———

"First Class seems boring to people sometimes, but it helps people to be aware of what goes on in most teenagers' lives."

———

"When and if students participate, it is a great way to let them know the good from the bad. Especially because the students get to teach and I think that they listen to them more because they have just, or are still going through, the high school hard times."

* * *

A FIRST CLASS LESSON PLAN FROM MUNDELEIN HIGH

The following is an example of a typical First Class topic sheet taken from the second year of Mundelein's program. The topic is the opening day assembly, which had long been a problem area at Mundelein.

COMMITMENT TO THE 3 RS

DURATION: 25 minutes

OBJECTIVE: To rekindle First Class commitment to the 3 Rs

MATERIALS: The lesson plan copies for all advisory members of "Why the Seniors Won."

PROCEDURE: Ask all advisory members to sit in a circle. (Figure out a way in your advisory meeting room to work this out.) Discussion will not take place if people are sitting in rows or with their backs to each other.

Ask the members to replay in their minds the opening day assembly on August 12, 1998.

Listen to the P.A. for the next instructions.

QUESTIONS FOR DISCUSSION

1. What was the purpose for being in our class groups? (see our friends, feel we belong to a group, yell for our class)
2. Why do we yell "The Battle Cry" in our class groups? (see which class can yell louder, have fun, to out-yell the other classes, to show class loyalty)
3. What is the purpose of "The Battle Cry"? (to show class and school spirit)
4. Why is the last part of "The Battle Cry" 'V-I-C-T-O-R-Y That's the Mustang battle cry'? (the last part is to show united spirit to inspire our teams to win)

5. At one point during "The Battle Cry," Mr. Davis asked some members of the sophomore class to stop yelling "Freshmen Suck." Why do you think some of the sophomores yelled that? (it's tradition)

6. Does yelling "Freshmen Suck" support the 3 Rs of First Class? Why or why not?

7. Does yelling "Freshmen Suck" support the purpose of "The Battle Cry"? Why or why not?

8. Some MHS sudents suggest that "The Battle Cry" be eliminated. What do you think? Why?

Hand out copies of "Why the Seniors Won."
Have everyone read it silently. It's in both English and Spanish.

Our next opportunity to yell "The Battle Cry" will be at the homecoming assembly. Which class do you predict will win "The Battle Cry" honors at the assembly? Put your prediction on a slip of paper and give it to your leader.

FINAL THOUGHT: Let's make 1998-99 First Class in every way.

* * *

Some Memos from the Early Days of Deerfield High's First Class Program.

DEERFIELD HIGH SCHOOL
TOWNSHIP HIGH SCHOOL DISTRICT 113
1959 North Waukegon Road
Deerfield, Illinois 60015-1807
312-432-6510
John A. Scornavacco, Principal
September 11, 1989

To all DHS Support Staff:
You may or may not be aware of a refreshing renewal at DHS. The entire teaching and administrative staff has become engaged in an effort to rekindle some forgotten values with the goals of creating a truly "first class" educational environment. To begin, we identified three problem areas to work on:

1. Offensive language and swearing in the hallways.

2. Excessive littering of the cafeteria and halls.

3. Everyone's right to dignified and respectful treatment by others.

Four separate workshops were conducted on the first Monday and Tuesday of school in order to share the outcomes that were suggested by a committee of teachers and administrators. Involved were strategies to get the whole school to invest in the improvement of behavior centering on the three points above. Because of time and optimal group size, we could not include everyone who, in one way or another, comes into contact with and deals with students. Hopefully the following information will convey the flavor of the direction we are following.

There is attached a copy of the paper all teachers used to open a discussion about the three problem areas. This was done in all first-period classes on the first day of school. The kids' reaction was invited during seventh-period classes. Feedback from staff is currently being requested.

During the workshops, the focus was on how to handle the students as we seek to change the school culture that they have become used to. We opted to pursue this in two ways.

1. Proactively—wherein you try to create a situation that addresses problems before they become large or out of hand.

2. Reactively—when a problem does arise, to try to handle it firmly but humanely.

With these two strategies in mind, what must occur is that everyone become involved and also be consistent. How we deal with kids must include the following:

1. Proactive Conditions
   - Kids are clearly knowing our expectations—tell them.
   - We will monitor behavior and not avoid problem areas.
   - There will be consistency, and misbehavior is accountable.
   - Problems will be addressed, not overlooked.
   - Solutions will be sought with student cooperation, not just legislated because we're the adults.
   - Positive reinforcement will be given for avoiding the escalation of a problem and solving it.

All these should be done in an effort to remind kids just what we expect them to be doing and to ask them to cooperate with us in building the best teaching climate. It helps if we talk with students other than for disciplinary reasons, since people with a positive social bond can cooperate more easily. It's not them vs. us, we're all in it together.

If, for one reason or another, the student will not allow a person in authority (all adult staff) to behave in a proactive, pro-social manner, then we may have to become reactive. The goal is to do it and maintain our own and the student's dignity.

2. Reactive Strategies

- Be nonadversarial; maintain a neutral tone.
- Maintain privacy and try to talk to the student by him-herself rather than in front of a group.
- Help someone if they're in need of a little support while dealing with a problem. Simply being there may be enough.
- Try not to appear as if you're getting "in a kid's face."
- Give yourself some room and work for the least level of reaction.
- Base this level on the intensity, duration, and frequency of student behavior in a given situation.
- Feel free to seek advice from a Dean or other staff member if you're not sure what to do.
- Use the Deans, if it comes to that.

Remember that your input is often as important and sometimes more important than that of a teacher. So, your investment in working with kids is really necessary if we are to achieve the first-class atmosphere we're after. There are no new rules and there is no crackdown. We just want to give our students every opportunity to work with us in achieving our goals and we will remind them when necessary. Hopefully, they will cooperate, but if they choose not to, the consequences will be administered as humanely as possible and not just an automatic punishment for particular behaviors.

Maybe you've noticed some change already, some of us have. If we continue to work on the three problem areas we've chosen and to let kids know we're personally concerned, things will get even better.

Thanks for your time in reading this and feel free to ask any of the following folks about anything mentioned in this communication.

*   *   *

May 31, 1990
To: DHS Faculty
From: First Class Committee

As the end of the school year approaches and things get a bit stressful, it becomes easy to forget or overlook things. One thing that should not be forgotten is the gain that has evolved with respect to the goals we set for ourselves in the fall of 1989. Admittedly, some retrogressive behavior has reared its ugly head of date, but we are still ahead of where we were at this time last year. You can still confront kids without "a lot" of sass, the halls are "fairly" clean, and kids are overall a bit more kind to each other than before. The applause goes to the staff for their initial investment. Hopefully we can muster the wherewithal to continue until the final curtain. The last act shouldn't spoil the show.

Next fall, "cultural lessons" will be brought to bear on the incoming freshman class in hopes of convincing them that DES does indeed have a touch of class. General expectations will be reviewed and optimistically some upperclassmen can be drafted to reinforce the faculty point of view with the freshmen. Plans are in the works to accomplish this.

Next fall we would also like to reengage the kids with some fresh approaches to our same (and maybe some additional) issues. In this, the folks who worked on the original "First Class" endeavors would appreciate some help. Please take a minute to jot an idea, a procedure, a focus point—any suggestion on a slip of paper and get it to my mailbox whenever you can. We'll be plotting and planning right after school ends. Thanks again for all your hard work.

August 27, 1991

TO: DHS Staff
FROM: First Quarter Cafeteria Supervisors
RE: First Class Expectations for the Cafeteria

While student conduct in the cafeteria has generally been acceptable, during our meeting yesterday we identified some behaviors essential to maintaining a pleasant atmosphere in the student cafeteria.

As you discuss the 1991-92 First Class Program in your second period class on Wednesday, August 28, please remind your students of these expectations for cafeteria behavior. Clarifying expectations is always helpful in establishing appropriate behavior.

Please remember that at Deerfield High School:

- We are courteous to all cafeteria employees, supervisors, and students.

- We place all refuse in the containers provided, we place empty trays on top of the containers, and we support the recycling program.

- We use trays for food, whether it is purchased at school or brought from home. We pay for food before consuming it. We don't throw materials or objects.

- We understand that tables are reserved for trays and study materials.

- We understand the importance of keeping food and beverages in the cafeteria. Students need written authorization to do otherwise.

cc: Teacher Aides

1/26/94

To: Classroom Teachers
From: First Class Committee
RE: Second Semester Kick-Off

A need has been identified to reintroduce, reinforce, and remind our students of the principles that have helped to make DHS a "First Class" school. We are asking all second-period teachers to take some time on Friday, January 28th to engage students in a discussion highlighting the following points:

- Reaffirm the accomplishments and cooperation shown by the students in the past regarding "First Class."

- Briefly review the four "First Class" principles.

- Discuss the importance of treating everyone with dignity and respect. We want to continue to raise student awareness in the areas of respecting and celebrating differences.

- Please also use this opportunity to discuss appropriate audience behavior. As we have a few assemblies coming up, now would be a good time to ask students to identify what constitutes a "First Class" audience.

- The goal of this discussion is to keep our students focused on the many positive contributions "First Class" has brought to our school culture, and to keep everyone actively involved.

- We feel that this is an important activity. Please try to engage all your students in this discussion. We appreciate the instructional class time you will be giving up for this activity, but feel strongly that it will benefit everyone.

- Please also let your students know that, as a way of showing the school's appreciation of their "First Class" behavior, the music played on the Union juke box on 1/28 will be free for students.

Thank you.

OPINIONS ON

CHARACTER EDUCATION

The following is a sampling of how journalists and educators around the nation have greeted the Character Education movement.

Character Education Can Transform
Students and Schools
By Charles C. Haynes
Senior Scholar/Columnist—The Freedom Forum
October 17, 1999

Most Americans will tell you that character education in schools is a good idea. According to pollsters, 90% of us want schools to teach core moral values. But what should "character education" look like? And more important, does it work?

Last week the nation got some compelling answers to both questions when the Character Education Partnership announced the 1999 National Schools of Character. The winners—10 schools and one school district—prove that effective character education programs can transform schools.

Take a look at Marion Intermediate School in Marion, S.C. Discipline referrals were down 50% in the first year character education was implemented. Each school year begins with staff and students setting goals related to good character. Then, for the next nine months, learning about core moral values is integrated into the teaching of history, literature, and other subjects.

Or go across the country to Youth Opportunities Unlimited in San Diego—a school for "at-risk" urban students. Once a war zone, the school now has the lowest suspension rate in the school district. What turned things around? Emphasizing and teaching core values in all school activities and throughout the curriculum.

Another winner, Traut Core Knowledge School in Fort Collins, Colo., is a charter school with a waiting list of 500 students. A strong focus on 12 core values throughout the school culture has contributed to high academic achievement at Traut Core. The school now ranks first in reading and in the top five in math out of the 26 schools in the district.

Private schools are also on the list. The Montrose School in Natick, Mass., has daily homerooms that focus on character discussions and leadership, and the school provides many opportunities for service to others. At Montrose, moral development is inseparable from academic achievement.

The district winner—Wake County Public Schools in North Carolina—is a case study in how to get comprehensive character education programs going in every school. Beginning in 1992, the district appointed a task force with broad representation from the community. Public meetings were held, surveys sent out, and other efforts made to ensure that character education in the schools would be built on the shared moral values of the citizens in this large and diverse district.

Today, character education is part of the mission of every Wake County school. The district provides in-service training and resources for teachers, encourages parental involvement, and evaluates the results.

Higher academic achievement, lower drop-out rates, fewer discipline problems, a more positive and caring school environment—who doesn't want schools like these? And who wouldn't like to see students who are more caring, respectful, honest, and responsible?

These award-winning schools help to dispel longstanding myths about character education. Myth one: "We can't agree about whose values to teach." Wrong. Myth two: "Character education can't be done without imposing or ignoring religious commitments." Wrong again.

The evidence is in. When schools and communities come together to consider character education, they are able to find consensus across religious and ideological differences about what to teach—and how to teach it.

Does your school district have a quality character education program? Is it being carried out in a way that is comprehensive and effective? If the answer to either question is "no"—or even "I don't know"—then maybe it's time to get to work. Teaching moral character and civic virtue should be at the heart of the mission of every public and private school in America.

For more information about how to get started—and about the National Schools of Character awards—contact the Character Education Partnership at www.character.org or call (800) 988-8081.

Your questions and comments are welcome. Write to Charles Haynes, The Freedom Forum First Amendment Center, 1101 Wilson Blvd., Arlington, Va. 22209. E-mail: haynes@freedomforum.org

* * *

Culture War and Schools:
Dangerous Directions
By William J. Moloney
Colorado Education Commissioner

What William Bennett described as America's "culture war" has gained new prominence by the recent controversy over the proper use of the National Motto, "In God We Trust."

The spark for this debate came when the Colorado State Board of Education passed a non-binding resolution encouraging "appropriate display of the National Motto in schools and other public buildings." Three weeks later the U.S. House of Representatives overwhelmingly passed a nearly identical resolution.

Given concern over the real dangers faced by school children today and the overwhelming support of elected officials, it seemed unlikely any reasonable person could seriously oppose these resolutions.

No so. Immediately following Colorado's action, the ACLU threatened to sue any school that dared to expose children to this dangerous kind of expression.

How strange that an organization devoted to defending freedom of expression should be so adamant in denying the people's right to express a sentiment accepted in our society for centuries and repeatedly upheld by federal courts.

This opposition is clearly reflective of a fault line among opinion-makers regarding the role of values in our society. As Bennett and others have pointed out, this conflict, if unresolved, has most serious implications for the future cohesiveness of our democracy.

The acknowledgment of a Supreme Being has always been embedded in our public life. From the Mayflower Compact to the Declaration of Independence, the Constitution and beyond, such references were near universal and unchallenged.

The Founding Fathers' idea of separation of Church and State was very simply that no one religion should be allowed to trespass upon the rights of any other. This in no way conflicted with their equally deep conviction that religion would always be the foundation of public morality, and as such, essential to the future well being of the new Republic.

So pervasive were these sentiments that our legal tradition ceased to view them as religious per se, but rather secular speech of a patriotic character.

"In God We Trust" was introduced to our currency under Abraham Lincoln and formally adopted as the National Motto under Dwight Eisenhower. All subsequent legal challenges to the National Motto have been rebuffed by the federal courts which defined "In God We Trust" as a form of "ceremonial deism" secular, not religious in character and having the purpose not of promoting religion but rather fostering patriotism and celebrating the national heritage.

Our nation's school children open each day by reciting the Pledge of Allegiance including the phrase "one nation under God." Also, one of the verses of the National Anthem says, "In God is our trust."

Those who would ban the Pledge of Allegiance, the National Anthem, and the National Motto in our schools are advocating an extremist point of view that can do enormous harm to our national life.

If our schools can be cleansed of all references to God, then the threat to our society, as a whole, is self-evident.

These advocates of thoroughgoing secularization sincerely believe that such a society would be a more "tolerant" place. Yet the last century gives examples of wholly secularized states—Hitler's Germany, Stalin's Russia—that should be sufficiently horrific to give pause to anyone dreaming of a new and better Secular America.

Among the growing numbers of people abandoning public schools, and the larger number wanting to but too poor to afford it, the most commonly cited reasons revolve around values.

As more parents come to see schools as "value-free zones" which undermine the values they seek to foster at home, then we are in serious trouble.

Virtually, the entirety of our population, whatever their faith, acknowledges God. Through history, our schools, like our society, have done so as well. This common bond has been a transcendent and unifying element in our nation's life.

If by tortured logic, we deny this heritage, we are attacking the sense of unity upon which our civil society depends.

History teaches us that traditions, values, and freedom itself are lost incrementally in a thousand careless little steps.

Let us reflect deeply, and then step back from this perilous path. All who care about the future of our children and our country will know how much is at stake.

Reprinted by permission from Colorado Education Commissioner William J. Moloney, a member of the Board of the Education Leaders Council. This article also appeared in the New York Times.

CHARACTER EDUCATION

INFORMATION

This is from a column titled "Character Education in the Public Schools" taken from The Freedom Forum's web page. The column has been updated with the help of the Character Education Partnership.

Character Education in the Public Schools
By Charles C. Haynes
Senior Scholar/Columnist—*The Freedom Forum*

One of the most significant areas of "common ground" for many Americans is the desire to have strong character education in the public schools. There is growing recognition across the religious and political spectrum that character education in schools must be an essential component of the effort to develop civic virtue and moral character in our nation's youth. The resources and strategies outlined [here], drawn from the work (guidebook) of the Character Education Partnership, will help communities translate an interest in character education into a plan of action.

CHARACTER EDUCATION AND CIVIC VIRTUE

First, a word of advice: Sound character education programs should be rooted in the democratic principles of the United States Constitution, the core civic values that bind America as one nation of many peoples and faiths. A strong commitment to these principles is crucial if we are to sustain and expand the American experiment in democratic freedom. Today the exploding ethnic and religious diversity of our nation makes it more important than ever that schools and communities reaffirm the obligations of citizenship that we share across our differences.

Properly taught, civic education in the United States is character education, because the strength of our democracy rests upon a virtuous citizenry. While the family and faith communities are primarily responsible for shaping moral character, the schools have the vital task of teaching and inspiring civic virtue. A central mission of schools has always been and must always be to transmit from one generation to the next the habits of the mind and heart necessary for good citizenship.

Civic virtue must be both modeled and taught in our nation's schools. When school policies and classroom practices reflect constitutional principles, students learn to respect the rights of others, even those with whom they deeply disagree, and they learn to take responsibility for the welfare of the school community. The civic framework of rights, responsibilities, and respect that we have discussed throughout this guide must be in place in all classrooms so that every lesson, whatever the subject, is simultaneously a civics lesson.

By teaching civic virtue and democratic culture, schools become training grounds for participation in the public square of America. Students not only learn about the public policy issues that confront our society, but also how to debate those issues with civility and respect.

Civility allows for vigorous debate over deep differences, using persuasion and not coercion, accompanied by a willingness to seek the common good. Through open and fair debate, students learn the value of democracy, but also understand the dangers of majoritarianism. A recognition of their own inalienable rights must be joined to a commitment to guard those rights for all others. A shared understanding of the civic virtues necessary for good citizenship is the starting point for achieving moral consensus in the public life of our nation.

CHARACTER EDUCATION AND RELIGION

Second, a word of caution: When schools and communities adopt character education programs, they must keep in mind that the moral life of a great many Americans is shaped by deep religious conviction. Both the approach to character education and the classroom materials used should be selected in close consultation with parents representing a broad range of perspectives. When care is taken to find consensus, communities are able to agree on the core values they wish taught in the schools and how they wish it to be done. The civic and moral values widely held in our society, such as honesty, caring, fairness, and integrity, can be taught without invoking religious authority. In public schools, where teachers may neither promote nor denigrate religion, these values must be taught without religious indoctrination. At the same time, teaching core values may not be done in such a way as to suggest that religious authority is unnecessary or unimportant.

Sound character education programs will acknowledge that many people look to religious authority and revelation for moral guidance. Such programs will affirm the value of religious and philosophical commitments, and avoid any suggestion that morality is simply a matter of individual choice without reference to absolute truth. Students will be encouraged to consult their parents and religious leaders for a fuller understanding of how their tradition addresses moral questions.

Character education can be hollow and misleading when taught within a curriculum that is silent about religion. When religion is largely ignored, students get the false and dangerous message that religious ideas and practices are insignificant for human experience. A complete education must of necessity include study about religion, where appropriate, throughout the curriculum.

Religion and religious perspectives are taken seriously in the curriculum if students are exposed to the great ethical systems of world history, and to America's rich and diverse religious heritage.

Mentioning religion is not enough. Students need to explore the place of religion in history, literature, art, and music if they are to understand the ultimate beliefs and world views that provide the deepest and strongest sources of human meaning for much of humanity.

CHARACTER EDUCATION PARTNERSHIP
MISSION STATEMENT

The Character Education Partnership is a nonpartisan coalition of organizations and individuals dedicated to developing moral character and civic virtue in our young people as an essential way of promoting a more compassionate and responsible society.

As our nation confronts the urgent moral challenges of the 21st century, it is imperative that Americans work together to develop the civic virtue and moral character of our youth. To do so is to strengthen the very fabric of our nation and to sustain the American experiment in liberty.

We recognize and affirm the primary role of the family in shaping the moral character of children, the vital task of schools in teaching and inspiring civic virtue, and the shared responsibility of each individual and community to model moral character and civic virtue.

By civic virtue, we mean living by the guiding principles of our nation's framing documents that are at the heart of our common compact as citizens.

By moral character, we mean living by core values widely held in our society such as caring, honesty, fairness, responsibility, and respect for self and others.

We are a compassionate society if we demonstrate in our life together an active concern for the welfare of others.

We are a responsible society if we guard the fundamental rights of all citizens and carry out the obligations of citizenship by working toward a common vision of the common good.

While we affirm our commitment to shared civic and moral values, we also recognize that deep differences exist on moral and social issues before the nation. We affirm, therefore, our commitment to address such differences within the civic framework of rights, responsibilities, and respect.

CHARACTER EDUCATION PARTNERSHIP'S PROGRAMS
AND ACTIVITIES

National Clearinghouse: Collecting and distributing information on educational and community programs designed to develop moral character and civic virtue.

Community Programs: Facilitating the implementation of character and civic development programs in communities throughout the nation by sharing information and resources.

School Support: Working with school boards, teachers, and administrators to initiate and strengthen comprehensive K-12 character education programs.

Publications: Disseminating information on successful character education programs.

Annual/Regional Forums: Bringing together experts and concerned individuals to exchange information and further develop effective character and civic programs.

National Awards: Recognizing exemplary programs in character civic education.

Public Relations: Raising public awareness of and increasing support for effective character and civic education programs.

TEACHER EDUCATION: ENCOURAGING SCHOOLS OF EDUCATION TO INCORPORATE CHARACTER EDUCATION IN THEIR TEACHER PREPARATION PROGRAMS

Membership in CEP is open to organizations and individuals sharing a commitment to developing moral character and civic virtue in youth. Annual dues are $30 for individuals and $300 for organizations, depending upon size. For more information, or to join CEP, contact:

Esther F. Schaeffer
Executive Director
Character Education Partnership
1600 K Street NW, Suite 501
Washington, DC 20006
Phone: (202) 296-7743 x10 or (800) 988-8081
Fax: (202) 296-7779
Web site: *http://www.character.org*
E-mail: eschaef@character.org

ADVICE FROM CEP: HOW TO START A CHARACTER EDUCATION PROGRAM

The Character Education Partnership (CEP) defines character as understanding, caring about, and acting upon core ethical values such as respect, responsibility, honesty, fairness, and caring. Developing character in this comprehensive sense requires, we believe, a comprehensive educational approach—one that uses all aspects of schooling (academic subject matter, the instructional process, the management of the school environment) as opportunities for character development. Above all, we believe, the school itself must embody character. It must be a moral community that helps students form caring attachments to adults and to each other. These relationships will nurture both the desire to learn and the desire to be a good person.

A question each school community must answer is: "What character education program should be used?" CEP believes that it is important for the parents and teachers of each school district to make that decision because "ownership" is vital to getting character education accepted in any school community. There is one caveat, however, and that is that the selected program should not violate society-wide values ensconced in the Constitution and otherwise widely shared. To facilitate the selection process, however, CEP has a data bank of programs that have been used successfully in different schools around the country from which a school community can select.

Although character is best developed by using all aspects of schooling as opportunities for character development, there are many ways to begin. Some schools start with commercially available "stand-alone" programs that require relatively minimal training of the faculty and staff. Other schools begin by trying to make a visible improvement in student attitudes and behavior in a problem area of the school environment such as the corridors, the cafeteria, or the playground. There is not a single script.

The stories of successful character education efforts reveal many ways to get a program started and to keep it growing. However, there are certain common denominators: leadership, an effort to get parents involved, time for staff to discuss how to emphasize the school's target values in all that the school does, and a more responsible role for students in acting upon the core values and solving real-life problems in the school environment. In the long term, each school should follow a plan of progressive integration of character education into all of the academic disciplines including staff development. In addition, each school should obtain a caring commitment from the principal through the custodians and bus drivers; i.e., the entire school should strive to become a moral, caring community.

ELEVEN PRINCIPLES OF EFFECTIVE CHARACTER EDUCATION

There is no single script for effective character education, but there are some important basic principles. The following eleven principles serve as criteria that schools and other groups can use to plan a character education effort and to evaluate available character education programs, books, and curriculum resources.

1. Character education promotes core ethical values as the basis of good character.
2. "Character" must be comprehensively defined to include thinking, feeling, and behavior.
3. Effective character education requires an intentional, proactive, and comprehensive approach that promotes the core values in all phases of school life.
4. The school must be a caring community.
5. To develop character, students need opportunities for moral action.
6. Effective character education includes a meaningful and challenging academic curriculum that respects all learners and helps them succeed.
7. Character education should strive to develop students' intrinsic motivation.
8. The school staff must become a learning and moral community in which all share responsibility for character education and attempt to adhere to the same core values that guide the education of students.
9. Character education requires moral leadership from both staff and students.
10. The school must recruit parents and community members as full partners in the character-building effort.
11. Evaluation of character education should assess the character of the school, the school staff's functioning as character educators, and the extent to which students manifest good character.

(CEP Material by Tom Lickona, Eric Schaps, Catherine Lewis, reprinted with the permission of the Character Education Partnership.)

FOSTERING CHARACTER EDUCATION IN LOCAL COMMUNITIES

(Advice from the Character Education Partnership)

1. Educate yourself about character education by reading books, journals, and other materials. Learn how character education has helped (a) reduce antisocial behavior such as violence, teen pregnancy, substance abuse, and disrespect for parents, teachers and peers, (b) improve academic performance, and (c) prepare young people to be responsible citizens and productive members of society.

2. Join national partnerships and networks to stay in touch with developments in the field of character education. The following groups will be helpful: (1) The Character Education Partnership, 1600 K Street NW, Suite 501, Washington DC 20036, 800-988-8081 or 202-296-7743; and (2) ASCD's Character Education Network, Center for the Advancement of Ethics and Character, Boston University, 605 Commonwealth Avenue, Boston, MA 02215.

3. Contact your local school officials to ask whether schools in your community provide K-12 character education, including community service learning. If so, ask to meet with the appropriate administrators and/or teachers to find out what local citizens might do to broaden public support for the program and enhance its effectiveness.

The following is published with the permission of the Character Education partnership from their publication "Building Community Consensus for Character Education," 1998.

IDENTIFY COMMUNITY LEADERS.

Key Issues

Strong leadership is critical to the success of any character education project. Good leaders are passionate about character education and possess the commitment, knowledge, willingness to learn, and perseverance needed to overcome any initial resistance. They know how to bring people together and create enthusiasm for bridging differences for a common goal.

Actions to Consider

1. Identify the educators, parents, business people, religious, and civic leaders who will champion this effort.
2. Identify leaders who have expressed interest in character education.
3. Identify groups interested in working with others in the community.
4. Determine the role you, as initiators, envision in this effort.

FORM A PLANNING GROUP THAT EMBRACES MANY COMMUNITY PERSPECTIVES.

Key Issues

The most effective character education programs are partnerships that bring together the talents of parents, school principals, school board members, teachers, students, business men and women, plus representatives of different faith communities and youth service organizations. Each of these groups is involved with the children and youth of the community in a different way, while sharing a commitment to developing personal and social responsibility in young people.

Actions to Consider

1. Determine where character education activities can take place.
2. Identify and contact groups which should be represented in the initial discussions.
3. Identify and contact individuals (e.g., prominent community members) who should be involved.

AGREE ON GROUND RULES FOR PLANNING GROUP DISCUSSIONS.

Key Issues

It is essential to the early success of the character education planning group that an open and enthusiastic forum for the sharing of ideas is encouraged. By agreeing on ground rules and guidelines for discussion that stress the importance of debating differing viewpoints with civility and respect, a healthy, more productive and creative environment will be assured.

Actions to Consider

1. Draft ground rules to promote planning, process development, and implementation in a respectful manner.
2. Make sure guidelines reflect the values of respect and responsibility.
3. Focus on issues and areas of agreement. Promote consensus. (Don't let side issues derail the process; set them aside for future consideration.)

ESTABLISH A COMMON CHARACTER EDUCATION KNOWLEDGE BASE AND VOCABULARY.

Key Issues

When a diverse group of individuals meet for discussion of a common topic, clear communication requires that everyone speak the same language. It is helpful, therefore, to define terms such as "character education," "moral," "virtue," "values," and "ethics." A value identified as "good character," for example, might mean different things to different people, but it is important for clarity of discussion that a common definition is agreed upon.

The planning group should review how other communities have defined character education and the different programmatic elements they have used. It is also helpful to look at research about how values are acquired by children.

Actions to Consider

1. List and define character education terms and definitions the planning group will use.
2. Identify questions that might be expected from community members. (See CEP resources for help with answers.)
3. Identify and investigate alternative character education approaches. (What has worked in other schools and communities?) Assess and build upon existing community support.

ASSESS AND BUILD UPON EXISTING COMMUNITY SUPPORT.

Key Issues

In some communities, character education may already be supported in schools and community programs for the moral development of young people. By listening to teachers, parents, students, coaches, and civic leaders attuned to school and community agendas, you can build on the best qualities of these existing programs.

Actions to Consider

1. Inventory character education efforts that are already in place.
2. Determine the most successful of the previous local character education initiatives and analyze why they have succeeded.
3. Identify potential sources of support and opposition.

IDENTIFY AND DEFINE CHARACTER TRAITS IMPORTANT TO THE COMMUNITY.

Key Issues

While there may be universally agreed-upon traits of good character and ethical values, each community will have unique core character traits it considers more important than others. The planning group will be challenged with identifying, defining, and illustrating these core traits, either through surveys, forums, or other methods of determining community opinion.

Core values adopted by communities often include such qualities as caring, honesty, fairness, responsibility, and respect for self and others. Whatever the values your planning group identifies, it will have to develop consensus about what the values mean in terms of behaviors that can be seen in the life of the family, school, and community.

Actions to Consider

1. Use consensus to determine what polling method (surveys, forums, etc.) will best identify the character traits most important to the community.
2. Brainstorm a list of traits the school and community should nurture.
3. Use consensus to select and define these community character traits and offer examples illustrating how they can be taught naturally throughout the school day, at home, and in the community.

DEVELOP A COMPREHENSIVE APPROACH TO CHARACTER EDUCATION.

Key Issues

Character education is most effective when it is woven into every aspect of every child's day at home, at school, and in the community; and it is even more powerful when what is taught in the schools is reinforced by the actions of the adult community. Academics, classroom instruction, athletics and co-curricular activities, school management and climate, staff development, parent involvement, and community service projects all provide rich opportunities for developing character in young people.

When character education is viewed as an ongoing process and not simply as another add-on to an already overcrowded school day, it truly takes root in the hearts and minds of students.

Actions to Consider

1. Review the CEP publication, "Eleven Principles of Effective Character Education."
2. Encourage business and government leaders to join in the process, supporting the schools and serving as role models for good character at work and in the community.

DEVELOP ACTION PLANS FOR EACH GOAL.

Key Issues

Once the group has chosen the core character traits and knows what it wants to accomplish, action plans can be designed to achieve key goals. It is vital also at the outset to plan for evaluation of both the implementation actions of the plan(s) and the overall results the community hopes to achieve through character education.

Actions to Consider

1. Identify and involve all segments of the community—students, parents, teachers, support staff, administrators, senior citizens, volunteers, business and civic leaders—in the development and design of the action plan.
2. Create strategies to introduce the character education initiative and character traits to these groups.

3. Develop plans to have each target group identify how they currently model or reinforce the character traits and suggest ways to improve current efforts.

4. Emphasize training for all involved.

5. Set clear, measurable goals.

6. Build evaluation into the plan by identifying benchmarks ahead of time that will indicate success.

GET THE BACKING OF YOUR LOCAL GOVERNMENT AND SCHOOL BOARD.

Key Issues

An official action of endorsement by the local municipal government and school board will give added public credence to your character education program. The endorsement can come early or late in the planning process. (Local officials sometimes prefer to see grassroots support for character education before they offer their blessings.)

Actions to Consider

1. Determine which government or bodies in your community need to endorse the initiative.

2. Find out what must happen before these bodies will endorse the effort.

3. Consider what form—mission statement, policy, or resolution—is preferred for the endorsement.

4. Seek the endorsement when it has the best chance of being received.

EXPAND COMMUNITY SUPPORT.

Key Issues

Active participation from all groups in the community is essential if character education is to become a way of life. Let the public know what the group is planning and involve them every step of the way. Encourage the community to support and build on what the schools are doing.

Actions to Consider

1. Get the word out about what the group proposes—the specific character traits it wants to nurture and how it has involved others in developing the plans to accomplish its goals.
2. Develop a strategy for early and regular communications with community members.
3. Prepare for questions and be open to further suggestions from the community.
4. Invite newspapers, television, radio, youth organizations, law enforcement agencies, parent organizations, religious leaders, and the business community to group meetings.

LOOK AT FUNDING ISSUES NECESSARY TO PUT PLAN INTO PLACE.

Key Issues

Some communities find they need resources beyond the school district's budget to carry out their vision for character education. Consider how to get financial support for training, materials, and activities from business, foundations, and individuals.

Actions to Consider

1. Begin to identify potential costs.
2. Identify potential funding sources for program expenses.
3. Determine additional needs for support beyond local government agencies.
4. Consider forming a nonprofit organization, perhaps in cooperation with other local school districts and other community groups, to raise money for the effort.

MAKE CHARACTER EDUCATION AN ONGOING GOAL.

Key Issues

Character education initiatives that are deeply woven into the fabric of school and community life—including curriculum and youth programs—have the best chance of long-term survival and success. A strategy that nourishes, sustains, and improves character education initiatives as a permanent part of school district and community missions will provide continuity despite organizational and civic leadership changes.

Actions to Consider

1. Develop a formal structure that nurtures the development, practice, and evaluation of a character education initiative over a 5- to 10-year period.
2. Invest in high-quality training for parents, teachers, administrators, support staff, and students.
3. Develop a plan that supports and enhances CEP's "Eleven Principles of Effective Character Education."

(Charles Haynes is a Senior Scholar with the Freedom Forum First Amendment Center.

Much of the information above was provided with permission by:
Character Education Partnership
1600 K Street NW
Suite 501
Washington, DC 20006
202/296-7743 x10 or 800/988-8081(phone)
202/296-7779 (fax)
http://www.character.org
eschaef@character.org)

ADDENDUM 6

CHARACTER EDUCATION

RESOURCES

The following is an extensive list of organizations that offer assistance in starting a Character Education program, along with their mission statements.

Association for Supervision and Curriculum Development
1703 North Beauregard Street
Alexandria, VA 22311-1714
Phone: (800) 933-ASCD (2723)
Fax: (703) 578-9600
Web site: *www.ascd.org*

ASCD, a diverse, international community of educators, is committed to forging covenants in teaching and learning for the success of all learners. It has published the November 1993 issue of *Educational Leadership*, devoted to character education; *How to Plan a Program for Moral Education*, by Merrill Harmon; and *Moral Education in the Life of the School*.

Center for Civic Education
5146 Douglas Fir Road
Calabasas, CA 91302-1467
Phone: (818) 591-9321
Fax: (818) 591-9330
E-mail: cce@civiced.org
Web site: *www.civiced.org*

The Center for Civic Education promotes an enlightened, competent, and responsible citizenry.

Center for the Advancement of Ethics and Character
School of Education
Boston University
621 Commonwealth Avenue
Boston, MA 02215
Phone: (617) 353-3262
Fax: (617) 353-3924
E-mail: CAEC@bu.edu
Web site: *www.bu.edu/EDUCATION/caec/index.html*

Founded in 1989, the Center for the Advancement of Ethics and Character builds on a few simple beliefs: (1) that character education is an essential and inescapable mission of schools and thus must be done consciously and well; (2) that the human community has a reservoir of moral wisdom—much of which exists in our great stories, works of art, literature, and philosophy—and that this treasure must be a regular part of schooling; (3) that the teacher is central to the entire enterprise and must be selected, educated, and encouraged with this mission in mind; and (4) that the most important task facing America's schools today is engaging children in our moral wisdom and aiding them in the formation of the enduring habits that comprise good character.

Center for the 4th and 5th Rs
SUNY Cortland
PO Box 2000
Cortland, NY 13045
Phone: (607) 753-2456
Fax: (607) 753-5980
E-mail: C4n5rs@cortland.edu
Web site: *www.cortland.edu/c4n5rs/*

The mission of The Center for the 4th and 5th Rs (respect and responsibility) is to help schools, families, and communities build good character in youth.

Character Education Institute
at California University of Pennsylvania
Educational Studies Department
250 University Avenue
California, PA 15419-1349
Phone: (724) 938-4500
Fax: (724) 938-4156
E-mail: huffman@cup.edu

The Character Education Institute at California University of Pennsylvania serves as a resource for the University's colleges, departments, and student organizations as they contribute to the moral development of students, and provides an outreach to local school districts and parents as they influence the moral development of their children.

Community of Caring
Joseph P. Kennedy, Jr. Foundation
1325 G Street, NW
Suite 500
Washington, DC 20005-4709
Phone: (202) 393-1251
Fax: (202) 715-1146
E-mail: contact@communityofcaring.org
Web site: *www/familyvillage.wisc.edu/jpkf/PUBLIC.HTML*

Community of Caring transforms the culture of a school to create a community of learners supported by a climate of caring and collaboration among staff, students, parents, and society at large. A Community of Caring where Caring, Respect, Responsibility, Trust and Family are taught and lived.

Council for Spirituality and Ethics in Education
1465 Northside Drive
Suite 220
Atlanta, GA 30318
Phone: (404) 355-4460
Fax: (404) 355-4435
E-mail: info@csee.org
Web site: *www.csee.org*

Understanding the search for meaning as universal and essential, the Council for Religion and Independent Schools supports that search as necessary to the nourishment of young people of conscience and community. The Council serves as a national resource for schools to encourage the moral, ethical, and spiritual development of young people. It promotes community service, provides resources and a network for schools' involvement in community service and service learning.

Educators for Social Responsibility
23 Garden Street
Cambridge, MA 02138
Phone: (800) 370-2515
Fax: (617) 864-5164
E-mail: educators@esrnational.org
Web site: *www.esrnational.org*

Educators for Social Responsibility is dedicated to helping young people develop the convictions and skills to shape a safe, sustainable, and just world. ESR promotes children's ethical and social development through professional development and instructional materials addressing conflict resolution, intergroup relations, and character education.

Ethics Resource Center
1747 Pennsylvania Avenue, NW
Suite 400
Washington, DC 20006
Phone: (800) 777-1285 or (202) 737-2258
Fax: (202) 737-2227
E-mail: ethics@ethics.org
Web site: *www.ethics.org*

The mission of the Ethics Resource Center is to serve as a catalyst to improve the ethical practices of individuals and organizations from the classroom to the boardroom. The vision of the Ethics Resource Center is an ethical world.

The Giraffe Project
PO Box 759
197 Second Street
Langley, WA 98260
Phone: (360) 221-7989
Fax: (360) 221-7817
E-mail: office@giraffe.org
Web site: *www.giraffe.org*

The Giraffe Project is a nonprofit organization that moves people to stick their necks out for the common good-by honoring real life heroes and telling their stories. The Project uses these heroes' stories and what is learned from them in a curriculum for schools that gives kids real heroes and moves them into brave, compassionate service themselves. There are Giraffe Heroes Programs for children in kindergarten-through-twelfth grades.

The Heartwood Institute
425 N. Craig Street
Suite 302
Pittsburgh, PA 15213
Phone: (800) HEART-10 or (412) 688-8570
Fax: (412) 688-8552
E-mail: hrtwood@heartwoodethics.org
Web site: *www.heartwoodethics.org*

The mission of the Heartwood Institute is to promote the understanding and practice of ethical values that are the foundation of community among all people, with particular emphasis on children and families and the understanding of seven universal attributes: Courage, Loyalty, Justice, Respect, Hope, Honesty, and Love.

The Hyde Foundation
616 High Street
Bath, ME 04530
Phone: (207) 443-5584
Fax: (207) 443-8631
Web site: *www.hyde.edu*

On a national scale, The Hyde Foundation seeks to create school communities with a child-centered philosophy and culture committed to developing the unique potential, character, and intellect of all children. These school communities embody a new partnership which: (1) eliminates the gulf between families and schools; (2) provides a challenging and disciplined school setting; and (3) instills character, confidence, and a drive for personal excellence in students, teachers, and parents alike.

Institute for Global Ethics
11 Main Street
PO Box 563
Camden, ME 04843
Phone: (800) 729-2615 or (207) 236-6658
Fax: (207) 236-4014
E-mail: ethics@globalethics.org
Web site: *www.globalethics.org*

The Institute's mission is to discover and articulate the global common ground of ethical values, analyze ethical trends and shifts in values as they develop around the world, gather and disseminate information on global ethics, and elevate public awareness and discussion of global ethical issues.

Jefferson Center for Character Education
PO Box 4137
Mission Viejo, CA 92690-4137
Phone: (949) 770-7602
Fax: (949) 450-1100
E-mail: centerjcc@aol.com
Web site: *www.jeffersoncenter.org*

The Jefferson Center's mission is to develop and provide curricula, programs, and publications that teach core values and ethical decision-making skills that foster good conduct, personal and civic responsibility, academic achievement, and workforce readiness.

Josephson Institute of Ethics
4640 Admirality Way
Suite 1001
Marina del Ray, CA 90292-6610
Phone: (310) 306-1868
Fax: (310) 827-1864
E-mail: CC@jiethics.org
Web site: *www.charactercounts.org*

The Josephson Institute of Ethics aim is to improve the ethical quality of society by advocating principled reasoning and ethical decision-making. Since 1987, the Institute has conducted programs and workshops for over 100,000 influential leaders; including legislators and mayors, high-ranking public executives, congressional staff, editors and reporters, senior corporate and nonprofit executives, judges and lawyers, and military and police officers. The CHARACTER COUNTS! youth education initiative is a project of the institute.

Learning for Life
1329 W. Walnut Hill Lane
Irving, TX 75038-3085
Phone: (972) 580-2000

It is the mission of Learning for Life to serve others, to instill values of good character, participating citizenship, and personal fitness in young people and in other ways to prepare them to make ethical choices throughout their lives so they can achieve their full potential.

National Association of Elementary School Principals
1615 Duke Street
Alexandria, VA 22314-3483
Phone: (703) 684-3345 or (800) 386-2377
Fax: (703) 548-6021
E-mail: programs@ naesp.org
Web site: *www.naesp.org*

NAESP is dedicated to ensuring every American boy and girl receives the world's best elementary and middle school education. NAESP recognizes an obligation to make continuing contributions toward strengthening the principalship and the profession.

National Association of Secondary School Principals
1904 Association Drive
Reston, VA 20191-1537
Phone: (800) 253-7746 or (703) 860-0200
Fax: (703) 476-5432
E-mail: nassp@principals.org
Web site: *www.nassp.org*

NASSP offers educators opportunities for growth and development and the resources they need to develop and manage effective schools.

National Council for the Social Studies
3501 Newark Street, NW
Washington, DC 20016-3167
Phone: (202) 966-7840
Fax: (202) 966-2061
Web site: *www.ncss.org*

NCSS is committed to engaging and supporting educators in strengthening and advocating social studies. Founded in 1921, National Council for the Social Studies has grown to be the largest association in the nation devoted solely to social studies education and serves as an umbrella organization for elementary, middle/junior and high school, college, and university teachers of integrated social studies as well as all of the disciplines.

Character Plus
Cooperating School Districts of Greater St. Louis
8225 Florissant Road
St. Louis, MO 63121
Phone: (800) 478-5684
Fax: (314) 516-4599
Web site: *http://info.csd.org*

Within the cultural diversity of schools there is a core set of values that all share. PREP models, teaches, and communicates these shared beliefs and values, e.g., responsibility, respect, humanity, honesty, self-esteem, and cooperation. As a result, students will adopt these beliefs and values as a part of their personal ethics and become positive contributors to society.

Phi Delta Kappa International
408 N. Union
PO Box 789
Bloomington, IN 47402-0789
Phone: (800) 766-1156
Fax: (812) 339-0018
E-mail: headquarters@pdkintl.org
Web site: *www.pdkintl.org*

The basic purpose of the League of Values-Driven Schools is to foster the development of positive beliefs and behaviors among students, teachers, administrators, and parents regarding the values of learning, honesty, cooperation, service to others, freedom, responsibility, and civility. Other values are important and should be fostered, but these special values will be singled out for regular attention and special emphasis in all league schools. The League is supported by the Sir John Templeton Foundation, the Gund Foundation, and the Phi Delta Kappa Education Foundation.

Quest International
P.O. Box 304
Annapolis Junction, MD 20701
Fax: (240) 646-7023
E-mail: quest@alink.com
Web site: *www.quest.edu*

Quest International's mission is to empower and support adults throughout the world as they nurture responsibility and caring in young people where they live, learn, work, and play.

*   *   *

RESOURCES FOR GETTING STARTED WITH CHARACTER EDUCATION

Amundson, Kristen J. "How to Institute a Values Education Program," *Teaching Values and Ethics: Problems and Solutions*. A Critical Issues Report. AASA, 1991.

Outlines specific steps a school or school district can follow in establishing a values education program: evaluating current policy, establishing a community task force, implementing and evaluating values activities and programs, and implementing a communications program. To order, contact: American Association of School Administrators, Publication Sales, 1801 North Moore Street, Arlington, VA 22209-9988, (703) 875-0730, Fax: (703) 841-1543. Cost $14.95.

Berkowitz, Marvin W. *A Primer for Evaluating a Character Education Initiative.* Character Education Partnership, 1997. Available from Character Education Partnership, 1600 K Street, Suite 501, Washington, DC 20006, (800) 988-8081, Fax (202) 296-7779.

This pamphlet is targeted at communities that already have character education programs occurring. It outlines the methodology of evaluating such programs and offers insights into how to keep the momentum.

Educational Leadership, Character Education Issue (November 1993). Available from Association for Supervision and Curriculum Development, Ordering Department, 1703 N. Beauregard, Alexandria, VA 22311-1714, 1-800-933-ASCD(2723). Cost: $5.00.

How to Establish a Values Education Program in Your School: A Handbook for School: A Handbook for School Administrators. Baltimore County Public Schools Task Force on Values Education and Ethical Behavior (1991).

Outlines steps for establishing a local values education program, including assessment of school priorities and students, and involvement of all parts of the school and local community in each phase of the development process. To order, contact: Office of Planning, Baltimore County Public Schools, 6901 North Charles Street, Towson, MD 21204, (410) 877-2063, Fax: (410) 887-4308. Cost: $2.00.

Kilpatrick, William. *Why Johnny Can't Tell Right from Wrong.* Simon and Schuster, 1992.

Lickona,Thomas. "Getting Started and Maintaining Momentum," Appendix A in *Educating for Character.* Bantam, 1991.

Outlines 15 steps from "Develop a Leadership Group" to "Evaluate the Program."

Moral Education in the Life of a School. A Report from the ASCD Panel on Moral Education. April 1988.

This report offers a useful framework for examining critical issues such as morality, religion, and achieving consensus on morality within a community. This booklet also offers 10 specific recommendations for educators to act upon. To order, contact: The Association for Supervision and Curriculum Development, 1703 N. Beauregard, Alexandria, VA 22311-1714, 1-800-933-ASCD(2723), ASCD Stock # 611-88038. Cost: $6.00.

Personal Responsibility Education Process Handbook and *Resources for Educators and Communities.*

These handbooks describe St. Louis's school-business-community partnership promoting character education and list effective programs and activities being used there. To order, contact: PREP, The Network for Educational Development, 13157 Olive Spur Road, St. Louis, MO 63141, (314) 576-3535, Fax: (314) 576-4996. Cost: $5.00 each.

Stirling, Diane. *Character Education Ideas for the School, Home, and Community.* PREP, 1998.

*   *   *

THE CHARACTER EDUCATION PARTNERSHIP BOARD OF DIRECTORS

Mr. Sanford N. McDonnell
McDonnell Douglas Corporation
c/o Boeing Company
P.O. Box 516
St. Louis, MO 63166-0516

Dr. Kevin Ryan
Director Emeritus, Center for the Advancement of Ethics and Character
621 Commonwealth Avenue
Boston, MA 02215
Phone: (617) 353-3262
Fax: (617) 353-3924

Dr. Eric Schaps
Development Studies Center
2000 Embarcadero
Oakland, CA 94606

Dr. Thomas Lickona
Center for the 4th and 5th Rs
Education Department
P.O. Box 2000
Cortland, NY 13045

Dr. Charles Haynes
Freedom Forum First
Amendment Center
1101 Wilson Blvd.
Arlington, VA 22209

Mr. David Fisher
President of Trust, Investments & Banking; Bank of America
800 Market Street
St. Louis, MO 63101-2506

Dr. Sheldon Berman
Superintendent
Hudson Public Schools
155 Apsley Street
Hudson, MA 01749

Dr. Diane Berreth
Deputy Executive Director
ASCD
1703 N. Beauregard
Alexandria, VA 22311-1714

Mr. W. J. Bowen
Transco Energy Co.
P.O. Box 1396
Houston, TX 77251

Ms. Kristie Fink
Character Education Specialist
Utah State Office of Education
250 East 500 South
Salt Lake City, Utah 84111

Mr. Thomas Kimble
608 Hawksmoore Court
Clarkston, MI 48348

Mr. Clifton L. Taulbert
The Freemount Corporation
700 N. Greenwood Ave.
Tulsa, OK 74106

Mr. Noel Moore
Sangamon Trading, Inc.
222 West Adams Street, Suite 2200
Chicago, IL 60606

Ms. Linda McKay
Director
CHARACTER*plus*
8225 Florissant Rd.
St. Louis, MO 63121

Mr. Paul Werner
c/o Conner and Chopnick
500 Fifth Ave., Suite 740
New York, NY 10110-0002

Mr. Jim Palos
Executive Director
Midtown Educational Foundation
718 South Loomis Street
Chicago, IL 60607

Mr. Forest Montgomery
Counsel, Off. of Public Affairs
NAE
1001 Connecticut Ave. NW
Washington, DC 20036

Dr. Marvin Berkowitz
Marillac Hall 469
School of Education
Univ. of Missouri—St. Louis
St. Louis, MO 36121-4499

Ms. Sylvia Peters
Enterprise Foundation
312 Martin Luther King Blvd.
3rd Floor
Baltimore, MD 21201

The information above was provided with permission by the Character Education Partnership:

1600 K Street, NW
Suite 501
Washington, DC 20036
202/296-7743 x10 or 800/988-8081 (phone)
202/296-7779 (fax)
http://www.character.org
eschaef@character.org)

INDEX